Longman Group Limited
London
Associated companies, branches and representatives
throughout the world

© Longman Group 1979

First published 1979
ISBN 0 582 20061 X

Printed in Great Britain
by Hazell, Watson & Viney Ltd, Aylesbury

Illustrations © Longman Group Ltd 1979
Cover photograph and photographs on pages 4 and 5:
Longman Photo Library
Text photographs by Lance Browne

Knockouts

Love at a Bus Stop

Janet Green

Longman

Bus & Coach

559478

Mark
Page 6

Dee Dee
Page 36

Mrs Etherington
Page 78

Bean
Page 108

Jennifer
Page 56

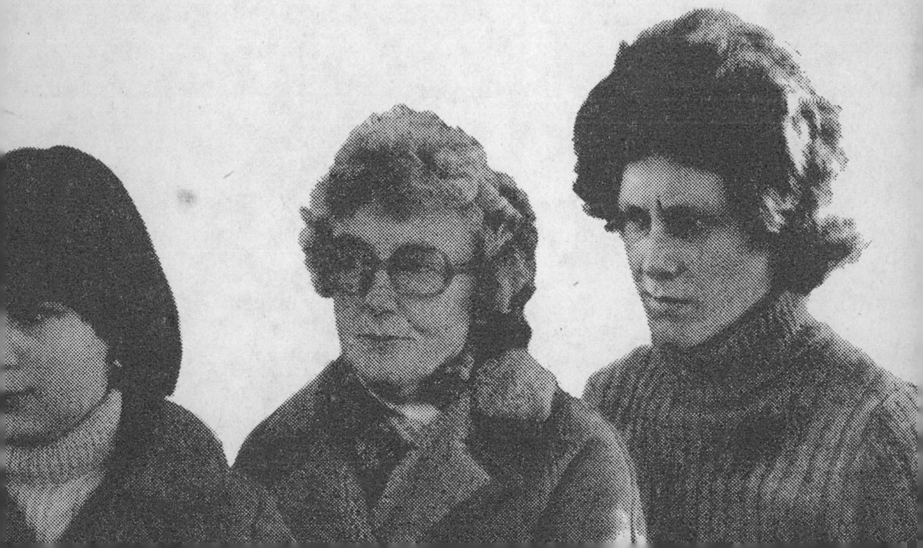

Mark

Mark

Every time I stand at a bus stop, I think of her. And I feel bad about it. Any bus stop will do. After all, when you've seen one bus stop you've seen them all – give or take a shelter or two.

The bus stop I'm thinking about was at the end of her school road, planted in a litter of tickets and fag ends. We all used to say they were stuck-up bitches at that school, because they were all girls, and they wore uniform. She looked good in hers though, standing there waiting for the late bus, clutching her school bag. She was always there on Mondays, Wednesdays and Fridays.

I used to see her on my way to the Supermarket.

A lot of us worked there after school. It was more like a social club.

But social club or not, I found I was thinking about her while I was stamping the prices on the tins. I even used to think about her when I was chatting up the bird at the bacon counter.

Then, when I got sacked after the Ben Hur chariot race with the wire trolleys, I still walked past the bus stop at the same time – and doubled back home at the end of the block.

I never knew what to do about it, though. All day, I'd work out an opening line. I was quite good at it, if the girls were sisters of my mates or there was a group of us. But I didn't know what to say or do for just me and her.

I used to daydream about sliding up in this smart car, and I'd change the make of car every time I thought about it. But that was a dead loss. Even if I'd got a car, even if I could drive, even if I was old enough to drive, I still couldn't think of an opening line.

Then I made the mistake of telling Flapper.

Of course, he was bloody stupid about it.

'It's easy,' he said, belting his chest, 'Just go up and say, "Me Tarzan. You Jane." '

He did the funky gibbon all round the classroom. Then they all knew.

''Ere,' Mick said, getting out his rotten snot-rag. 'I'll lend you a hanky. Drop it and say, "Yours, I believe" . . .'

'If it was, I wouldn't want to know,'

I snarled.

'Well, a pen then,' he said. 'Drop it and . . .'
Flapper interrupted.

'That's too drawn out,' he laughed. 'Just
say, "Drop 'em!"'

He looked at me. He could see I was
getting annoyed.

'We're wasting our time, lads,' he said,
looking up at the ceiling. 'He thinks it's for
stirring tea!'

They went on about it so much that I
stopped going that way for a whole week — till
it died down.

Then on Monday, I started my bus stop
patrol, again.

I was so pleased to see her that I smiled.
And she smiled back!

On with the show. On the Wednesday, I tried,
'Hi.'

There should have been a sentence to
follow, but my throat clammed up. I don't
even know if she answered. I rushed past too
fast to find out. In fact, I was nearly past her
when I'd said it, so she probably thought I
was talking to somebody else, anyway.

That night, I paced it out in my bedroom.
How far before the wardrobe to say, 'Hi,' so
as to leave just enough time to get an answer,

but not long enough to have a long walk if I didn't. Trouble is, wardrobes are so silent. So, I tried 'Hi' on Flapper in the corridor at school. He just stared at me, and treated me like an outcast for the rest of the day.

I didn't get a chance on the Friday, 'cos she had a friend with her. A girl. I knew the score. Try it then, and I'd exit to a chorus of giggles. She didn't even notice me creeping past. That booted my confidence in the backside.

By the time the next Monday came round, I'd decided to start from scratch. It was my day for the non-committal smile.

It had about as much effect on her as it had had on the wardrobe. When I tried it later in front of the mirror, I realised why. Not only was it half-way between a grimace and a leer, but I'd got a lump of licorice allsort stuck between my two front teeth!

It was Wednesday again.

That night, as luck would have it, Flapper tagged on, and the trouble with Flapper is that he's so hard to lose. No side roads to slip down, either. Nothing for it, but to go on.

He was doing his hopping along the kerb routine. On off, on off. I've never seen Flapper walk straight down a street. He prefers walls to pavements any day, but as this row had fences he had to make do with the kerb.

'Try walking on your hands,' I said.

'What's it worth?' he said.

That's another thing about Flapper, he never knows when he's not wanted.

There were two of them at the bus stop again, but nobody else. We were getting nearer ... The secret smile routine? And nearer ...

I opted for having a deep conversation with Flapper, and not seeing anybody else. But it's hard to have a conversation with a kangaroo.

'Stop mucking about,' I said, having sudden visions of him hopping all over the girls.

When he reached the bus stop, they shot away from him like spat out chewing gum. He didn't even pause. He just took the post by the waist, swung round it, then shinned up it in one long movement. As the laws of gravity caught up with him, he scrabbled with clock-work legs, then he let himself slide smoothly down the post till he collapsed in a heap on the ground. That's another thing about Flapper. He's made of rubber — except for the wood in his head.

The girls were laughing. Then I twigged. He knew them. The whole routine was for their benefit. But he didn't introduce us. So we stood there – me and the bus stop – while he carried on performing like a one man band, and they giggled their approval.

At last, the bus rolled up. It hadn't run him over, though I wished it had.

The driver had about as much good manners as Flapper. He hardly stopped to let the girls get in. Flapper leapt on after them. A few yards further on, he jumped off again, then ran down the street after it, laughing his head off, and shouting, 'Mother, don't leave me!' to some old bag who was glaring out of the back window.

It turned out that the other girl was called Lorraine, and her brother had been at Flapper's junior school. My girl – well you know what I mean – she was called Mary. I'd never given her a name in my mind, but if I had, it wouldn't have been Mary.

It came as a shock to find out they were only third years. I wouldn't look twice at third years in our school.

By Friday, I'd decided to take the bull by the horns. There was no friend and no Flapper, so I knew my luck was in.

I marched straight up to her and started on my script.

13

'Hello, Mary,' I said.

'Hello,' she said, 'Where are you going?'

That floored me. I hadn't been allowing her any words. Certainly not questions.

'Er . . . um . . . nowhere in particular . . .' I replied, but seeing how stupid that sounded, I added, 'I go there every night.'

We stood there in an awkward silence.

'There's only three days in my week,' I said, launching into the next bit of my speech. 'Mondays, Wednesdays and Fridays.'

She looked at me as if I was half-cracked.

'There's seven in mine,' she said.

'No, I mean . . . what I mean to say . . .'

And then her mate arrived. Just in time for the bus.

'That old cat,' she puffed. 'Keeping me in just for a little thing like that.'

'What happened?' Mary asked.

'That Sister Ursula didn't like my hair.'

She'd had it permed into an Afro.

'She's says to me "Have you got no pride in yourself?" Honestly, what a stupid question! Just shows what *she's* like. So I asked her if she had any pride in *her*self. Well, of course, she sort of humphed — you know the way she does, so I told her a thing or two. "I dress like this," I said, "and I wear my hair like this, because I happen to like it," I said, "and I happen to think you're a sight," I said. So she kept me in. Just because she doesn't like my hair. The fat pig!'

I was getting a new insight into their snooty school. I just stared. Lorraine noticed me.

'Oh, hi,' she said, and explained that some of their teachers were nuns.

The bus rolled up, just as one of Flapper's jokes flashed into my mind.

'Hey,' I said as they clambered up, 'Why don't you tell the bus driver that he gets ten points for a nun?'

Mary looked at me blankly.

'If he runs over one. A nun,' I added.

Lorraine turned, and capped it dryly.

'And twenty points for a pregnant nun on a zebra crossing.'

She'd heard it before.

I thought of leaping on the bus like Flapper, but with my luck I wouldn't be able to get off. I contented myself with waving after them.

They weren't looking, but I got a lovely glare from the lady on the back seat.

Then it was the week-end. A whole week-end in which to revise my script. I spent most of the time day-dreaming. I had this fantasy

about saving her from drowning. But I can't
swim – so I settled for *her* rescuing me.

By Monday, no action of mine had got me
nearer to asking Mary out, but something else
happened which at the time I didn't understand at all, but which later, I came to understand only too well. This first year stopped me
in the corridor. A little girl, with little eyes like
pebbles.

'You know Lorraine Edwards, don't you?'
she said.

Her eyes didn't blink, and she stood there
like she was growing out of the ground.

'Who?' I asked, looking round, and feeling
very uncomfortable.

'She's my cousin,' she said.

'Oh.'

She kept on staring at me, and I actually
felt sorry for her teachers.

'Lorraine says Mary Evans wants to go out
with you.'

I sort of grunted.

She carried on staring at me. A shapeless
mess of little girl.

'Thanks,' I said and started backing away.

I went up the stairs, along the corridor and
down the next stairs rather than walk past
her, and feel those beady eyes boring into my

back. At ground level, I glanced back along the bottom corridor. She was still there, watching for me to come down the stairs. I gave her a weak little smile, and escaped out to the playing field.

My heart beat in my ears through the football match. I wasn't playing for Rovers this week, as I hurtled up the wing. I was rushing to rescue Mary from every TV plot I'd ever seen. I dribbled the ball past Martians, Gladiators and Superspies.

I was tackling a two-headed Vampire to protect her honour, when I got this kick in the shin. The mud rushed up to meet me, and that's when Flapper trod on my nose. It wasn't broken, though, and as soon as they found out it wasn't, everybody thought the whole thing was a scream. Some of them thought it was, anyway.

'I couldn't do that again if I tried,' Flapper laughed.

I'd got a beautiful black eye. A real shiner. The sort you'd be proud of – if you weren't going to try and chat up a bird.

But I needn't have worried. I didn't get anywhere near the bus stop. The games master drove me home in case I'd got concussion, and once I was in my bed, it would have been easier to get out of Colditz.

On Tuesday, Flapper called round. He was off from school suffering from that rare disease called French Test Tomorrow. It needs two days' treatment, so it's not so obvious. That's why I was still at home on Wednesday — I'd caught it from him. Besides which, I needed the time to think as a result of the news that Flapper had brought with him.

We'd been invited to a party.

'That Lorraine Edwards,' he said.

He was playing it cool, just bouncing on the bed instead of swinging from the lightbulb. I realised he was waiting to see how I'd take it, with her only being a third year.

'What did she say?' I asked.

'She didn't. This first year came up . . . a little girl . . .'

'I know the one,' I said.

I could see her. Eyes like press studs. From the look on both our faces there was no doubt we were thinking of the same little monster. Even Flapper had met his match.

'Will Lorraine's friend be there? Er . . . Marion . . . er . . . no . . . Mary?' I asked.

I don't know what I did wrong, but he stopped bouncing, and looked at me.

'You sly bugger,' he said. 'So that's the girl

you were on about!'

Flapper gave me some advice, then.

'You're playing it all wrong,' he said. 'She says she likes you, right? Well, keep her guessing then! Give the bus stop a miss for a day or two. You'll be seeing her on Saturday at the party, anyway.'

So on Wednesday I just lolled around playing some Andy Williams records that belonged to my mum. She took that as a sign I was having a relapse. But all the time, my eye was on the clock. In three hours Mary'd be at the bus stop. In two hours she'd be at the bus stop.

Not that I was going to go to the bus stop, of course.

Half an hour. Twenty minutes. I was going to keep her guessing.

Quarter of an hour.

I was going to play it cool.

Ten minutes.

With only five minutes to go, I threw on my coat, dodged past Florence Nightingale, hurtled out of the door, and belted down the street. The wind was shouting 'Mary' in my ears.

There were some steps — a short cut. As I flew up them, it was like going the wrong way on an escalator. It seemed longer running to that bus stop than it had ever done walking.

I saw the bus when I was on the last stretch. I was too late. She was getting on.

I waved frantically.

She was just about to sit down, when she looked back and saw me. She waved. I was so caught up in it, that I blew her a kiss. Except she didn't see it, 'cos she'd sat down by then. The only person who saw it was the lady on the back seat. I was building up quite a relationship with her.

It was Saturday. The day of the party.

Three-thirty seemed a bit of an early start. None of the girls at our school would've had a party at that time. Still, we were ready for anything. In fact, it seemed quite a good idea to start early. Saturday afternoons can be a bit of a drag.

I was still smarting over missing Friday. The French master had caught on at last. Flapper and I had to stay in and do the French test!

But the golden hour was arriving. Any minute now, I'd walk in the room and there she'd be.

Then I got an attack of stage fright. Yeah,

there she'd be, and what the hell would I say to her? I turned to Flapper in a panic. He was hopping along quietly to himself, working on fancying Lorraine, because it seemed too good a chance to miss. But he was keeping his options open though, just in case.

'How many birds do you think there'll be?' he asked.

'How should I know.'

'The more the better,' he said, and jumped on a small wall we were passing.

He shouldn't have said that. It was tempting fate. How were we to know that if you went to a girls' school, you weren't likely to know many boys?

We rang the bell, and the door was opened by the last person in the world that either of us wanted to see — apart from the French master.

She stood there, her inscrutable little eyes like black dots. They get friendlier characters answering doors in horror films. You couldn't outstare her, either.

But it went from bad to worse. They were *all* girls at the party. You couldn't really count Lorraine's ten year old brother and his friend.

'Where's your Richard?' Flapper asked,

when Lorraine came to say hello.

It turned out that her older brother had gone off somewhere. He'd got sense.

You've never seen such a collection of girls. Some were tarted up in party dresses with frills. Even little Pebble-Eyes had a ribbon in her hair.

I got the feeling that some of them had never seen a boy before. Perhaps they hadn't, going to that school of theirs. Or perhaps the ones they'd seen, hadn't lived to tell the tale!

Mary hadn't arrived yet, but a fat girl was giving us the eye. She advanced. Flapper and I looked at each other.

'Let's get out of 'ere,' we said.

But it was too late. Lorraine's mum bustled in and pushed a parcel into Flapper's hand.

'Get yourselves into a circle,' she said. 'Hurry up. We'll play Pass the Parcel before tea.'

We obeyed like people in a trance. The fat girl wobbled over. She walked like a Womble, and was one of the few of them wearing make-up.

Now, another thing about Flapper is that he likes fat girls. I've often heard him say, 'Cor, fancy being in the middle of all that!' But he didn't rate this one.

This gash of lipstick spoke.

'Budge over,' she said, standing in the middle between Flapper and me, and forcing a space for herself.

It was like Samson pushing down the pillars.

'A rose between two thorns,' she said, and smiled coyly at each of us, in turn.

The others had joined the circle, and we were wedged in. He'd got Pebble-Eyes, and I'd got something I thought resembled a zombie. With her white face and red dress, she looked like Manchester United.

And then Mary arrived.

She was carrying a little parcel which Lorraine's mother took from her, and put with a pile of parcels on a small table. Flapper caught my eye. For a minute he'd thought we were going to play Pass the Parcel all night! Then we realised they were presents. That made us feel even worse. After all, it was Lorraine's birthday.

We passed the parcel to a record from the *Mary Poppins* film. I didn't dare look at Flapper. I'd never known him to be so still in his life. He was as dead as a cold boiled egg.

I couldn't make Lorraine out. She stood watching the game, one minute looking as if she despised the whole thing, and the next, she'd be giggling and squawking like the rest.

It was the giggling that nearly finished me. I swear I could hear it echoing in my ears for a whole week.

We didn't get a look-in at the parcel. Pebble-Eyes deliberately by-passed Flapper, and the fat girl grabbed the parcel from me so fiercely that I nearly lost a finger. Even the zombie sprang to life like she'd had an electric shock. It was like being in the middle of an all-in wrestling match.

I kept out of it as much as I could, and looked for Mary. She'd disappeared in the kitchen to talk to Lorraine's mum. Sensible girl.

The tea was all right, though. A bit fiddly — napkins and all that stuff, and blowing out candles — but all right.

I was sitting next to Pebble-Eyes who had an uncanny aim with jelly. The little brother on the other side wasn't much better. My black eye had mellowed to a dirty yellow, and when Pebble-Eyes wasn't flicking me with jelly, she'd turn in her chair and stare at my eye.

Flapper was sitting next to Mary. They were getting on like a house on fire. I'd been making for the chair on the other side of her, but the fat girl had beaten me to it. You don't quarrel with the likes of her.

In the general confusion after tea, Lorraine and Mary made for the kitchen. Flapper followed them, and I was close behind. And behind me was Lorraine's mother.

'You two girls go back and organise the treasure hunt. It's nice of the boys to offer to wash up!'

We looked at all the plates.

Flapper has a knack for getting out of things. I could see his look coming on.

'If you're going to try the broken arm or the sprained wrist,' I said, 'I warn you, this lot will amputate. At the neck.'

We did manage to get a quick word with Mary and Lorraine, though. At the door, as we left!

But even there, Pebble-Eyes' beady currants stared at us.

She spoke.

'What you doing?' she asked.

'Shut up,' Flapper said. 'I'm just raping your cousin.'

Flapper and I went home.

I walked. He hopped.

'What do you think of Mary?' I asked.

'She's a half tidy bird,' he said, doing a

detour twice round a lamp-post.

'She'd be too quiet for you,' I said.

'Come off it,' he muttered, 'I don't want to pull your stupid bird, anyway. What's with you? Bet I could jump that wall.'

'Bet you can't.'

He could.

'Do you fancy Lorraine?' I asked.

'I wouldn't have dated her for next Saturday, would I, if I didn't? Next Saturday it'll be you and Mary, and me and Lorraine.'

I'd just been making sure.

'Tell you what though,' he added, 'We won't be going to no bloody parties!'

There was still a Monday, a Wednesday and a Friday to cope with. Monday was a non-starter, because Flapper came. He turned up on Wednesday too, because Mary said Lorraine would be there. But Friday I had her to myself.

I stood there as silent as a salt cellar.

'Where's Flapper?' she asked.

That put the lid on it. We just stood around looking silly. The only things I managed to say came out like gobbledy-gook. But Saturday made up for it all.

We'd arranged to meet in town. Flapper was full of beans. He was wearing his scarf

turned inside out at the end to make a hat, as
well. As soon as we met, Lorraine grabbed
the loose end of the scarf. It was a Rovers
scarf, the longest I'd ever seen. His sister got
carried away when she knitted it. Flapper
called it his Rovers Return.

The girls supported City so there was a bit
of pushing and shoving, and walking on the
opposite sides of the pavement chanting
'Rovers, Rovers,' 'City, City.'

I was hoping there'd be another session of
shoving. I didn't really get in on the first one,
except for an elbow in the ribs from Lorraine,
and I was pretty sure I hadn't touched Mary.
Both of them had pummelled Flapper like he
was a rag doll. And he loved it.

I was getting irritated with Flapper, but I
had to admit he was brilliant in the stores.
Swing doors and escalators are made for
Flapper. For an 'encore' he shouted 'Fire!' in
Woolworth's.

It drizzled in the afternoon, and we sat ages
in a Wimpy Bar, betting on raindrops, and
putting salt in each other's coffee. Nothing
special happened, but I remember every
minute.

Not that I understood everything.
Especially Lorraine. I couldn't figure her out

at all. There was no doubt it was Flapper she was after, but every now and again, I could have sworn she was making eyes at me. It made me feel uncomfortable, because I didn't really like her. And I got the feeling Flapper was going off her, too.

When we'd first sat down, he and Lorraine had made a big thing out of Mary and me sitting together. It was what I wanted, but it makes you feel awkward. But when the girls went off arm in arm to the lav, Flapper slid in by me. He stayed there when they came back. They didn't seem to notice, and they just slid along the opposite bench together, sniggering.

When we'd spent up, and Flapper had run out of tricks to do with the sauce bottle, and the guy behind the counter had got fed up with us, we decided we'd better walk home.

The rain had stopped, but there were plenty of puddles, and Flapper made the most of them. But he splashed Lorraine's coat, and she began to get bitchy. For a minute, I thought it was all going wrong. Lorraine grabbed Mary's arm, and the two girls went and walked ahead.

'Stuck-up bitches,' Flapper shouted.

Lorraine turned her head and stuck her tongue out.

'Sticks and stones,' she said, 'And I'm not inviting you to any more of my parties.'

Flapper was dribbling an empty Coke can down the road.

'I don't want to go to any more of your stupid parties,' he bawled, giving the can an extra special kick. It took off in their direction. It didn't go anywhere near them, but Lorraine let go of Mary's arm, and pelted down the road towards us.

One look at her face was enough. Flapper was off back down the road as fast as his legs would carry him. He was actually running in a straight line!

I looked towards Mary, took a deep breath and carried on walking.

'Don't let's bother about them,' I said.

First lines aren't so hard after all.

From the moment I got home, I re-lived those hours together. Even to seeing the dead cat on the side of the road, its guts squashed out like toothpaste. She'd shuddered, and I'd put my arm round her, and we'd stayed like that till the end of her street.

'Why Mondays, Wednesdays and Fridays?' she'd asked.

It was funny to think she'd been examining

29

every word, too.

Sunday, Flapper came round.

'Did she catch you?' I asked.

'You bet,' he grinned. 'I walked her home. Went down the park, first. Got into a bit of a grope. How did you get on?'

'OK,' I said. 'When you seeing her again?'

'You must be joking,' he said, and did a divebomb off our settee.

Monday, Pebble-Eyes gave me a letter. Flapper got one, too. He made it into a paper plane.

'You know,' he said, 'I'd like to go to that party again.'

'You what?'

'Yeah! Only this time I'd take my itching powder and my plastic dogdirt.'

My letter just reminded me she'd be at the bus stop. As if I'd forget. In the afternoon, Flapper didn't come in. Somebody had stuck a piece of rhubarb in the French teacher's exhaust pipe. So I thought Mary and I would be free, but we weren't, 'cos Lorraine was at the bus stop, too. I made excuses for Flapper, but he didn't bother to come on the Wednesday or the Friday, either. So after that Lorraine gave up.

That Saturday, Mary and I went to town

by ourselves. That was the first time I'd kissed her. I'd been thinking about Flapper's park all week, and by that night I'd found one of my own!

I don't know what happened to the Mondays and Wednesdays after that. I know I still went to the bus stop but I don't remember any particular incidents. It's the Fridays I remember. And, of course, the Saturdays.

Then one Friday she said:

'You don't have to come to the bus stop every time.'

I remember the panic. It threatened to throttle me.

'Don't you want me to?'

She smiled.

'I just didn't want you to feel obliged.'

'I want to see you,' I said, and, God, I meant it.

On the Saturday, we spent hours sitting on a bench in the park.

She talked.

I talked.

She told me about herself when she was little.

I told her about me when I was little.

She told me about her school.

I told her about my school.

She told me how she first noticed me.

I told her how I'd first noticed her.

Then we ran out of words, and it was dark enough, so we kissed.

The next Friday we couldn't stop smiling at each other. I knew she was thinking about next day, on the bench in the park. The funny thing is, I know we went there that day, yet that's another of the times I can't remember clearly.

I remember the next Friday though. That's when she told me she was going to babysit, and we arranged how I'd creep in. And I remember what we did, all right.

I don't think I'll ever forget the touch of her flesh. We were on the rug together in front of the fire with the lights off. She lay there with her eyes closed, and I remember holding my breath as I unfastened her blouse. I leaned over to kiss her. She was trembling.

'Are you cold?' I asked.

She turned her head away, and stared into the fire.

'You don't think I'm cheap, do you?' she asked, quietly.

I kissed her gently as my answer, then cuddled her in my arms.

'I wish we could stay like this forever,' she

whispered. 'Just like this. To sleep with our arms around each other.'

I knew just what she meant. No, I'll never forget it. The kissing, the cuddling, the caressing. And then the panic, when we heard a car outside. It wasn't the people of the house, but the spell was broken. So we just sat up and talked again.

I was glad we hadn't gone all the way. Though I told Flapper we had.

I wasn't seeing as much of him lately. He told me he wasn't bothering with girls any more. That was a mug's game, he said. He wasn't getting tied down to any bit of skirt.

'Love 'em and leave 'em,' he said.

The next Friday she told me she was baby-sitting again.

The previous week I'd seen her in the afternoons as usual, but this week was different. I went instead with Flapper to a cricket match. Neither of us can stand the rotten game, but it was our school team, and there was a chance of a bit of bother among the supporters. We weren't disappointed. A great afternoon was had by all. I don't know who won the cricket, or where the teams were going the next week, but the supporters were coming back for a return match! The Games master and the

French master ran the cricket, so mucking up their afternoon was an extra bonus for us.

When I crept in to share the babysitting, she was pleased to see me, but she was also peeved about the afternoon.

'Well if you're fed up of going to town,' she said, 'We can go somewhere else. We can go swimming.'

That was the last thing I wanted to hear.

The funny thing was that there'd been a time when I would even have done that. I'd have done it just to see her in a swimming costume, but there didn't seem any point now.

'Oh come on,' I said, and put my arms round her, nuzzling my mouth into her neck. I didn't kiss her, because she was still talking.

And that's when the blasted baby woke up – a fat jammy baby squelching in its nappy.

She was good with babies – I'll give her that, though she got embarrassed when it pushed its mouth against her breast.

'I'd like to do that,' I said, to ease the awkwardness, but it only made things worse between us.

Also the wretched kid just wouldn't shut up.

'We'll have to ring them,' she said, bringing our evening to an end.

And then that next Friday — at the bus stop — broad daylight — a few people in the queue. The bus comes. Mary turns — leans up and kisses me — and something about it made me think of stamping tins in supermarkets. That plum-coloured lipstick. Like dried blood. It wasn't tarty. I suppose it was fashionable — but not all over my face.

I finished it off gradually.

She was upset. But she never understood that I was upset, too. It's hard to accept that you can change like I did.

Dee Dee

Dee Dee

'Now, Deirdre,' my father was saying, 'If you know anything — anything at all — it's your duty to tell us.'

Well, I can tell you, it was touch and go. I wanted to blurt it out. To tell it how it was, and maybe if he hadn't called me 'Deirdre' I might have done.

All right, I know it's my name, but usually I'm Dee to my family — Dee Dee to my friends. Deirdre is for solemn occasions. End of term reports. Being caught smoking. Cheeking my mum. But then, I suppose, death *is* a solemn occasion.

'Well, Deirdre?' he prompted.

The words seemed to come from a different planet. I looked at him. It was a change from staring at the carpet.

We were in the front room. The early evening light slanted in through the window, and outlined my parents. With the light behind them I couldn't see their faces.

Mother was sitting slightly in front of the table on a hard-backed chair. Whenever we had visitors, she brought it into that position from its home against the back wall by the stereo. Dad sat solid in his armchair by the fire.

The visitor — an auntie, perhaps, or the vicar, or the insurance man — always sat on the end third of the settee. This time the visitor was a teacher, Miss Carter. One of the real old cows of our school. She was balancing a cup of tea and a plate with two semi-sweet biscuits on it.

There was another easy chair, the twin of my father's, at the other side of the fireplace. Nobody ever sat there — even when the visitors came in twos.

I was aware of that easy chair. If only they had asked me to sit down, I might have felt I could tell them. I wanted to tell somebody.

As if conscious of my thought, Miss Carter raised her hand slightly and said:

'Sit down, dear.'

But it was too late. I saw it for what it was.

'All they need now,' I thought, 'is a hard and soft team of policemen. One to beat the truth out of me, and one to wheedle it out.'

But I did so want to tell somebody.

39

'Oh, what the hell,' I thought again, and sat down.

Mother was feeling out of place and uncomfortable. Suddenly she flurried from her seat, and brought a small mock-regency circular table from the corner, and placed it by the settee arm. Miss Carter placed her teacup and plate on it. We all watched the movement as if it was important. Then she brushed a crumb from her skirt, and gave me her attention again, with a professional smile.

'We know Cynthia was your closest friend,' she said.

That so accurate use of the past tense upset me. Trust Miss Carter to get her grammar right. Cynthia was already something in the past.

And I didn't even know if it was true: that I'd been her friend. I didn't even know whether I liked her or not. We just hung around together.

'I told her not to mix with that girl,' my mother said, as if the point had some relevance.

Maybe it had. Perhaps that's why I went with Cynthia that fateful night.

I met her on my way to the disco. She was getting off with two boys who'd drawn up in a car, and I got roped into going to this party with them all. I didn't realise till later that she'd never met them before. They seemed nice boys, though, especially one of them.

I sneaked a look at my mother. She would hit the roof if she knew. And my dad! It wouldn't be the roof he'd be hitting.

Miss Carter was trying again.

'Now, Deirdre . . . without wishing to distress you . . .' she began.

To my humiliation, I felt tears begin to prickle at the back of my eyes. She hurried on.

'It's just that Cynthia always seemed to be such a lively girl . . .'

That's not the way she'd put it on school reports!

'She was so . . . er . . .'

Surely Miss Carter wasn't stuck for words. It wasn't that hard to remember 'Noisy, inattentive and disruptive'. Cynthia had been very proud of that report.

'So . . . er . . . so full of fun,' she said, finally.

I wondered if she was thinking about the wastepaper basket over the door. 'Fun' had been the very last word in her vocabulary then! Mother had folded her arms. She had her own opinion about Cynthia. She opened

41

her mouth, then thought better of it, and went to switch on the light.

And what did *I* think of Cynthia?

I found it hard enough to picture her face. I remembered her new wedges. I'd been jealous of those. My mother had said shoes like that were all right for those who wanted to break their necks, or injure their backs. I could see the make-up, but there wasn't any face.

And then very clearly I placed a mannersim. That habit she had of hitching up her bra straps tight, so her boobs stuck out like humps. It made me feel as flat as a pancake. And I think she said that to me once.

I wondered what Cynthia thought of me. I don't know why she latched on to me. I don't know why she bothered. She always made me feel that she'd 'been around' even when she wasn't boasting about it. And she had. She'd got a reputation. And she lived up to it.

I remembered something with a sickening flash. A group of us in the bogs, wondering what boys saw in Cynthia. I'd even been thinking on those lines that night on the way to the disco. I suppose she was 'boy mad', as my mother would say. But aren't we all?

I found myself looking at Miss Carter, but I was seeing her simpering up to the woodwork master. I wondered if she'd ever been to a party like that one. I'd never been to one like it before. My parties had all been jelly and paper hats.

Miss Carter was looking at me. I couldn't quite place the look, and I wondered why she was interested in Cynthia's death. It wasn't as if she liked Cynthia. She couldn't stand her. It was common knowledge. She was probably glad that Cynthia was dead. Except that she'd have to find somebody else to pick on.

It was Dad's turn to get in on the act. He stood up. He was fiddling with his pipe. Pressing his thumb into the blackened bowl.

'I didn't really know the girl,' he said.

The words came from a triangular patch of mouth by the pipe's stem. A sucking wheeze gurgled round the room.

'I wish I'd known her better,' Miss Carter added, piously.

'A bit late now,' I thought.

It was if she'd rehearsed the next bit.

'And the mother can't throw any light on the situation. All her life before her. Everything to live for. So young.'

Then came my mother's voice.

'Don't bite your mouth, Deirdre.'

I was remembering Miss Carter telling

Cynthia that she'd never make anything of her life.

'Sorry, Mum, I was thinking about Cynthia,' I said.

They all looked at me, in an ecstasy of sympathy. It made me want to puke. Then they did a chorus of 'So young,' 'How sad,' and 'It makes you think.'

Mother's solo which started, 'Not to say ill of the dead ... but ...' was interrupted by Miss Carter's rendering of, 'In the midst of life we are in death.'

I was more interested in whether they would bury her with her wedges on, but they were all set for a session on the wastefulness of it all, and, of course, on The Future.

My parents are always getting hung up about The Future. As if where you're going matters more than where you're at.

Cynthia hadn't cared a fig for things like that. The only writing she did was on walls and desks. To her, school was a joke. She only bothered to turn up so she could make up to the boys. All the boys knew her. The girls used to get catty. But she didn't seem to care about that. They could say what they liked. She'd turn her nose up and walk on – as if she was proud of herself. Yet nobody kept up their grudges against Cynthia.

I shivered.

Mum automatically drew her cardigan edges closer, but she finished her sentence before she lit the gas fire. The words hung on the empty air after she'd moved.

'. . . and that's what I always say to our Deirdre. And to our Stephen before he went into the Navy.'

'That's probably why he went into the Navy,' I thought.

I hadn't caught the beginning of the sentence, but it was certainly true that she was always saying *something*. But it was never a conversation.

The slurp of Dad's pipe was joined by the hiss of the gas fire. The hissing grew in the ears of my memory and it was Cynthia whispering.

'Don't talk about school you stupid idiot. They think we're at least sixteen.'

Luckily the only person who might have heard us was too busy necking. Then, the two boys came back with our drinks. They hadn't asked us what we wanted. And it wasn't in glasses. Just in cups — cracked ones, too.

They never asked anybody if we could come into the party. But it was so dark, I suppose you couldn't tell who was there. We weren't far from where we live in fact — not if you cut across the golf course — but there wasn't likely to be anyone there we knew. It was a grown-up's party, I decided. Not like the dinner and dance my parents had gone to that evening, though.

Cynthia went to find the loo. Denny put his arm round me. He started nibbling my neck. I sat ever so still and felt really odd inside. Then he stopped, sat back and whistled between his teeth.

'Jesus,' he said, 'I've got a right one here.'

He turned to his mate, Chris, who was sitting next to him like a spare part.

'This one's like a Fairy Liquid bottle,' he said.

I thought he meant my shape, and I wanted to cry.

'Don't snivel, for God's sake. All I meant, babe, was your plastic resilience — Give us a hug — Boing! Give us a kiss — Boing!'

He was wafting his hands, as if he was being reasonable. But I couldn't understand the way he talked, and I felt miserable. He was nice looking, too.

'Jesus, I could do with a drink,' he said.

I was going to tell him he'd got one, but he

knocked it back in one gulp. As he got up and passed his mate, I could hear him talking, sort of to himself, but it was for Chris, too.

'So I says, "Let's go and find a bit of spare," I says . . .'

By the time he came back, Cynthia was there too. She made a space for him next to her. Within seconds they were well away. The two of them in the middle of the settee, with Chris and me like sentinels at either end.

I looked at the settee in our front room. Miss Carter was sitting in the same position as Chris had been. But there the resemblance ended.

Hiss, the gas fire murmured.

Tap, tap, tap. Dad was mucking out his pipe again.

On another plane of existence, the conversation was playing like a cracked record. They'd even started answering *for* me the questions directed *at* me.

'I hope you're feeling better yourself, Deirdre,' Miss Carter said.

'Yes, thank you, she'll be back in school tomorrow,' my mother said.

That was news to me.

'Just a chill on her tummy. You know how these things are.'

47

In fact it had been a king-size hangover.
Not that Mum realised.

'I was sorry you had to hear the news over
the telephone.'

'Yes. Such a shock.'

'Yes. Dreadful shock.'

The word 'shock' seemed to lose its
meaning, the more they used it.

The clock went 'Boing!' – or more like
'Burp', it being an old clock.

I'd been clock-watching at the party.

The clock was a battered antique, half
hanging off the wall. Or maybe I wasn't
seeing straight, although I hadn't had all that
much, really. Well, not like the others, but it
went straight to my head.

I knew I was safe till one o'clock, though.
I knew my parents wouldn't be back till then,
and normally I'd hate to miss out on a chance
like that, but to be honest, that night I wanted
to go home.

Then Denny and Cynthia wandered off to
some bedroom somewhere, with her looking
so smug – as if she'd proved something. Chris
moved to sit by me.

'Denny's all right,' he said. 'You can't
blame him trying it on.'

'And you? Are you all right?' I asked,

putting the lid on it for a while.

We sat in silence. Things were hotting up around us. It was getting like musical chairs. Except there were no chairs. And no rules. The settee was like a little island. We got invaded gradually, at both ends, till Chris and I were wedged together like two upright books. We were the only people sitting up in the whole room.

He shifted slightly and put his arm round me. It was a sensible thing to do really – it was far more comfortable – but it sent butter-flies pounding again.

'I'm only fourteen,' I said.

But he wasn't listening. There was something on his mind.

'Look,' he blurted out suddenly, 'You're very nice and I like you a lot. It's no reflection on you. It's just that there's this girl see. She lives in Croydon . . .'

'That's fine by me,' I said. 'What's her name?'

And then it was like we'd known each other for years. Somebody once said that I was a good listener. I think they must have been right. It was fun then. He wasn't handsome or anything, but he grew on you, he was good company.

He held my hand as he took me home across the golf course, and I looked anxiously at the house when we got home, but everything was OK. I'd got back before them. At the gate he stood and looked at me.

'I'm glad it turned out the way it did,' he said.

Then he kissed me gently. I was in the house before I realised that I'd left my bag at the party.

Tap. Tap. Tap.

Dad was indicating that he was back in the conversation.

'Have any of the other girls been able to throw any light on it?' he asked.

'No. Not at all. We can't think why she would have done such a thing.'

'She wasn't . . . er . . . um. She wasn't . . .?'

'No. She wasn't.'

The tight-lipped expressions of both my mother and Miss Carter said the rest. A teacher had once said she was 'free with her favours'. We'd had hysterics.

'I had a little heart to heart with some of the girls.'

Miss Carter actually said 'gels'. She always did. Cynthia could take it off to a T. She'd have loved that whole sentence. I'd missed the

50

little heart to heart of course, but I could imagine the dramatics.

'It will be fairly straightforward at the coroner's court.' Miss Carter continued. 'I'm glad really that none of the girls will have to be called. It's not . . . nice.'

She had a special way of saying that word, too.

'Well, our Deirdre's a sensible girl. I'm sure she would have said . . .'

'Quite.'

I was fascinated by the way she said those little words. But it didn't stop me noticing the relief in her voice, and I was amused.

Then something suddenly clicked in my mind. So that was Miss Carter's angle! What a gas! It was so flaming obvious when you stopped to think about it, too.

Did she really think that she'd driven Cynthia to it? With that petty bullying? God, Cynthia would have loved that. She'd have had a ball! I cleared my throat, and they all looked at me.

I was tempted to play cat and mouse with her. But somehow, it seemed pointless. And anyway, maybe I was wrong. After all, it was far fetched. Or was it? I didn't know.

I could feel her eyes on me. They were all

waiting for me to speak. I stared at her bag.
And, in my mind, there I was, by that other
doorway again.

My bag was in my hand. I'd had to roll a
sleeping drunk out of the way to get it. The
windows had all been thrown open, but no
kind of air stood a chance against the putrid
stench of alcohol, vomit and stale tobacco
smoke.

I guessed Cynthia was there somewhere.
Her mum was on nights, and when I used to
listen to her adventures, I'd envied the
freedom that had given her.

But it was Denny I saw first. He was
rinsing his face in water at the sink. He looked
the worse for wear. I felt rotten myself, and
not up to talking. Then I realised Chris must
be in there, too. There was a smell of coffee
brewing. The tinkle of the spoon sounded like
a sledge hammer, and over it, I could hear
Chris talking. I didn't want him to see me. I
was frightened he'd think the bag was an
excuse. I was just turning to go when Denny
started talking.

'Christ Almighty,' he said. 'I must have
been bloody plastered. I must have been out
of my mind.'

He was blowing water all over the place, as

he was talking.

'I opened my eyes – and Jesus, it was some effort – and there was this god-awful bird next to me. She's probably even worse when she's awake. A real scrubber . . .'

There was a lot more. Hell, such a lot more. And he hadn't seen her, standing at the other door.

I was looking into her eyes. But she didn't see me. She wouldn't have seen me, if I'd been standing right in front of her.

I ran.

I didn't want her to know that I'd seen that ripping, tearing, stripping, shattering pain in her eyes. Oh, it wasn't shame, or hurt. It was . . . loss.

I ran. I keep telling myself that I did the right thing. I keep telling myself that I'm not responsible for what she did. How was I to know she'd go and do something like that? I knew she was upset, but I thought she'd get over it. I never thought she'd do anything like that. It wasn't as if she was like Gina. Gina's always going to commit suicide – if she's not in school, she's having the stomach pump.

But, Cynthia wasn't like that. We all thought she could take it.

My mother was talking.

'People should keep tablets out of the way of children.'

I sighed as the room came back into focus. Miss Carter was still looking at me, as if I was going to say something. She leaned forward and touched my knee.

'You can tell *me,* my dear,' she said.

'I'm sorry, Miss Carter,' I said. 'I don't know anything about it.'

Jennifer

The first part of the plot was a suitcase.

There was a nest of suitcases on top of my parents' wardrobe. The little one would do the trick. I took it from inside the others. Then I put the rest back on top of the wardrobe. I made sure I put them the wrong way round so the handle was facing the wall. Mother was bound to notice. She never missed a thing.

I tip-toed back to our room, and slid the little case under Maddy's bed.

There was no danger of Maddy finding it. She never did any cleaning. She wouldn't recognise a Hoover if she saw one.

That's the trouble with older sisters — they're bone idle. Maddy treated me like her personal slave. And it was no good complaining to my mother.

'It'll be your turn some day,' she always said.

That was a real stupid remark. How could it be my turn? I haven't got any younger sisters. And I can't see the cat doing odd jobs for me! Nor wearing my cast off dresses!

Maddy was still pigging her breakfast downstairs. Mam and Dad were down there too. So I tiptoed back to their room to try and imagine how long it would be before anybody noticed the suitcases. I pushed them slightly crooked just to be sure.

'Hurry up, Jennifer. You'll be late for school!'

Mother's voice made me freeze like an ice lolly.

'OK,' I mumbled, hoping she wouldn't be able to tell where the voice came from.

I waited till I heard her go back into the kitchen before I set off downstairs.

As Maddy and I left for school, Albert stalked in. Albert is the cat.

Mam was going to have a matching set: Albert and Victoria. Anybody who's met Albert can understand why she thought better of it. He's a huge pompous tabby with a wail like an injured Siamese — and spiteful, too. Dad says that Albert has an eye for the main chance. That's because Albert only comes in around mealtimes, sits wherever he pleases, and bites anyone in range. He doesn't go in for being stroked, and if he rubs against your leg, it's best to move out of the way.

That morning it was Maddy's turn.

'Stupid cat,' she said, rubbing her ankle and looking at the tiny hole in her tights.

'Fetch the nail varnish, Jenny. Transparent. It's on the ledge.'

It wasn't worth a row so I didn't argue, and anyway, I was going to get my own back.

'Nice Albert, puss, puss, puss,' I whispered as I strode over him.

He likes to sit halfway up the stairs. He hissed at me, but I didn't mind. At least Albert was one character who didn't distinguish between older and younger sisters.

Walking to school with your elder sister really cramps your style. Mother said it was good that we went to the same school, because I wouldn't be bullied. But I'd rather be bullied once in a while than picked on by my sister every day.

She started as soon as we got out of the house.

'You look a state this morning. Shut the gate behind you. Stop scuffing your feet.'

She used to treat me like a pack horse. That morning it was her airline bag she wanted carrying. It had been raining the night before. That meant there'd be a puddle at the end of our street. With a bit of luck I'd manage to trail the corner of the bag through it. That cheered me up, so I started hopping along the edge of the kerb.

'Stop showing me up,' Maddy said. 'Walk properly.'

As we turned the corner, Malcolm joined us. He did that every day.

'Hi, Maddy,' he said.

He didn't even smile at me. They walked ahead. I paddled through the puddle dragging Maddy's bag, and thinking how different it had been the first time he joined us. He'd looked at me, and said:

'You're one of my first years, aren't you?'

I'd nodded.

'I'm her form prefect,' he'd said to Maddy. 'Are you her sister?'

She'd smiled, and he'd carried both our bags.

At the school gate, Julie Foster and three of our class had seen us. He borrowed my pen in registration to write up the merit marks. All day I got asked questions about him. On the second day, he gave me a boiled sweet. I kept it for weeks, until the paper fell off, and it took root in the fluff in my blazer pocket.

A car horn hooted. It was Dad going past

like he did every morning. Maybe it was him
going past every day that had given me the
idea in the first place. Or maybe it was
Malcolm's weekend job.

I smiled to myself and trailed along behind,
kicking Maddy's bag.

I walked alongside Malcolm to the
classroom. It was an effort to keep up with
him.

'I've got some new shoes,' I said.

But he didn't seem to want to know.

It was his job to get us in line. The class
used to play up a bit, but they liked him. Julie
Foster asked me if it was true that he was
going out with my sister.

'No chance,' I said.

They'd asked me that a lot lately. I could
never decide what line to take, and what there
was in it for me.

'Honest?' asked Julie. 'Cross your heart?'

She gave me a sweet.

'Well . . . he likes her . . .' I said.

I took another sweet, gave her a mysterious
smile, and slid into the room.

It was true he liked her. He ought to have
had more sense. And Maddy? She couldn't
care less. She liked boys who'd left school.
They had more money. But she was stringing

Malcolm along, even though she didn't want him, like she did with anything in trousers.

I lent Malcolm my pen to do the merit marks, and smiled at Julie Foster. Then I went on the homework rounds. I got my pen back so I could make my French match everyone else's.

'My pen's run out,' I said to Malcolm.

His mate had popped in for a few minutes. They were talking. Malcolm turned to me.

'Well run after it then,' he said.

That really sealed his fate.

It hadn't taken Mother long. We were sitting at the table having tea. She asked Dad first, and simply got a mumble from behind the newspaper. She took that to mean 'What suitcase?' and turned her attention to Maddy.

'Where's the suitcase? The little one. Madeleine, I was asking you a question.'

'Oh, sorry, Mum. Suitcase? Dunno.'

Maddy went back to pigging her tea.

I knew exactly how to play my part. At the first mention, I'd stopped eating and looked up all bright and interested. I turned my head to look from one to the other. From Mother, to Dad's newspaper — from Mother to Maddy — and back to Mother again. I deliberately lifted my spoon before I asked brightly:

'Are we going on a trip, Mother?'

'No. Eat your tea.'

She caught sight of my spoon.

'And don't hold your spoon like that.'

I shrugged.

Dad had looked up from behind the paper.

'Do as your mother tells you.'

It had worked like a charm. Nothing else was said about the suitcase. The moment had passed. But Mother was looking puzzled, and I knew she and Dad would talk about it later.

When I went up to our room, Albert was already stationed halfway on the stairs. He followed me, and for once, I didn't encourage him to sit on Maddy's bed. When she arrived I started on the next part of the plan.

It had cost me a chunk of my pocket money to buy the chocolates. I took them out of my satchel before I started sorting out my homework. Albert stalked round the satchel, bit at the strap, then climbed among my books. Usually I booted the whole lot when he did that, but this night I talked to him gently, and helped him build a nest out of my French books. I knew the suspense would be too much for Maddy.

'Where'd you get those?' she asked.

'School,' I said 'Where d'yer think I'd get books?'

'The chocolates, idiot!' she snapped. 'Did you nick 'em?'

'No,' I said. 'I wouldn't be stupid enough to nick something as big as that. I nick chalk, not blackboards.'

I thought for a minute I'd gone too far, but it was all right. She was doing her best to smile. It was the be-nice-to-little-sister routine. What with her and Albert, the purring was getting a bit much.

'I'll tell you what,' I said. 'Let's have some music.'

I could have asked for a full scale disco and she would have agreed.

'I fancy something a bit quieter,' I said, after looking through her records as well as mine.

'I tell you what. I'll just pop down and borrow some of Mother's. Can I say they're for you? You know what she's like.'

So I went, and again it worked like a charm.

'Can Maddy borrow some of your records?' I asked. 'Some love songs. You know, yicky stuff like Andy Williams.'

I was as quick as I could be, because

Maddy holds the world record for stuffing chocolates.

I slammed the lid on the box as soon as I got back upstairs.

'Don't pig them all,' I said. 'Leave some for when we watch telly.'

Albert heard me putting on the record player. An evil-eyed glint showed through his bundle of fur. Usually it was scratch and run when the music started, but that night he must have thought his luck had changed. Sleepy music specially for cats. He fluffed out his furry cheeks, closed his eyes, and purred like a machine gun. I looked at Maddy. It was her turn now.

'Could you use some help with your homework?' she said.

That was a laugh. I could probably do hers better than she could. All this politeness was suffocating. I stuck it for half an hour. Then I led the way downstairs – the box under my arm, and Maddy close behind me.

Albert overtook us halfway down. He felt he'd done enough to ruin his image for one night, so he nipped my ankle on the way past. It was as good a place as any to hand over the box.

'Here,' I said. 'You might as well have

them. I feel a bit sickly.'

In the living room, I sat looking at the cartoon page in the paper. Maddy remembered her manners and offered Mother a chocolate. She was safe there. Mother was always slimming.

'Where did those come from?'

'They're Jenny's,' Maddy said, through a mouthful of chocolate caramel, and with her eyes glued to the telly.

I didn't say a word. I just looked up from the newspaper with my best blank expression.

I played exactly the same trick with the flowers the next day. Six red roses.

'Flowers?' Maddy said, when Mam asked about them. 'In our room? Oh them. They're Jenny's. She won them.'

I didn't say a word. I was getting really good at that blank expression.

The next day was Thursday, and it struck me that if I was quick, I could set it all up for the weekend.

As we left the house I said to Maddy:

'In a minute you'll be seeing loverboy.'

'Don't be stupid,' she said. 'Here, hold my tennis racket. And don't play with the press.'

'He's sweet on you,' I said. 'Everybody knows it.'

Saying that nearly choked me, but it did the trick, 'cos when he joined us, she remembered to give him an extra dose of the batting of the eyelids. In addition, that little conversation set everything up for the next time the phone rang for her. Two birds with one stone!

The phone rang at tea time.

'One day, I'll train Albert to answer that phone,' I said, trying to go at my normal snail's pace to answer it.

'Maddy, it's for you,' I yelled, bouncing back into the kitchen. 'It's loverboy Malcolm Rawlings.'

I didn't give her time to show any expression.

'It's all right,' I said. 'It's only Sarah.'

'Pig,' she said, as she went past me to the phone.

'Some people just can't take a joke,' I said to nobody in particular.

'Who's this Malcolm then?' Mother asked, carefully, as she dished out the jelly.

'Malcolm? Oh 'im. 'E's sweet on our Maddy,' I said. 'Dad knows 'im. He passes us every morning. Don't you, Dad?'

They were so busy looking at each other that neither of them noticed me push Maddy's plate nearer the edge of the table. She hadn't quite finished her corned beef. Albert is partial to corned beef.

I left the table nearly as fast as Albert did, and followed him upstairs. It was time to write the letter.

Malcolm was climbing up the wrong tree, if he thought he was getting any nearer with Maddy, but you couldn't blame him when you saw her flirting with him.

The next morning I walked along behind them, fiddling with the screws on the tennis press, and thinking about wastepaper baskets. Any minute now, Mam would be emptying the basket in our room. There was nothing in it except a letter carefully burnt. The letter was a mound of ash but for a tiny fragment down one side. A tiny fragment with a few telling words. Words like 'love', 'together forever', and 'can't wait till Saturday'.

In school, Malcolm walked along the corridor next to me. It was quite like old times. He was really being nice to me. I was glad I reminded Maddy to keep him on a string.

'You still doing your Saturday job?' I asked, as if I didn't know.

'Oh, my window cleaning job,' he laughed.

69

'Yeah, why?'

I sighed with relief. Time stood still while I waited for his answer.

'I was hoping you could do me a favour,' I said.

'Might. What is it?'

I explained what I wanted him to do. As soon as I mentioned our house he leapt at it like Albert leaps at corned beef. He was falling so easily for everything I said, that I almost felt sorry. I felt I'd have to give him a chance just to ease my conscience.

'After all your other calls,' I said.

'And if you're not too tired,' I said.

'And if your boss wouldn't mind,' I said.

'And if it's not too much bother,' I said. 'And if you're not going anywhere special.'

But the more chances I gave him to get out of it, the more he assured me he didn't mind.

'That's fine,' he insisted. 'What's up? Don't you want me to do it?'

'Yeah,' I said, feeling uneasy again. 'Only I can't afford a lot. Will it cost much?'

'For you darlin', nothin'. Don't worry about it. I'll do it just for you,' he said.

I nearly scrapped the whole idea there and then, but he went on to ask:

'Will Maddy be there?'

70

'Yes, she'll be there,' I said. 'But you don't think it's a stupid sort of surprise do you? I mean, if you think it's a silly idea, just say so.'

It was his last chance.

'No of course it isn't,' he said. 'It's an ace idea.'

'It's meant to be a present for my mother and father, so I'd rather pay you something.'

'A bag of crisps at break,' he said, with a smile.

That was easy. I'd get two bags of crisps for letting Julie Foster into the latest news. I wonder how many bags of crisps it would have been worth if she'd known the truth!

I didn't bother cribbing anybody's homework. We'd got that French back from the other day. Everybody had got it wrong. I would have been the only one with it right, if I hadn't altered it! I was glad I'd let Albert make a nest out of my French books.

I sat through registration looking out the window, and wondering if I should go through with it. I knew it would work. It had been almost too easy. Maybe I should knock the whole idea on the head. Mind you, I needn't go through with it. Even at the last minute, I could change everything. It was up to them.

Saturday morning.

I heard my mother and father talking.

'There's probably nothing in it. You're making too much fuss.'

'Look, Jim. Flowers and chocolates for a start. Jenny's! I ask you!'

'You mustn't underestimate our Jennifer,' Dad said.

I smiled until I heard the end of the sentence.

'She's a devious little madam. Too clever by half. It's not good in one so young.'

'Now Jim, you're getting off the point.'

'Well if you're worried about Maddy, why don't you ask her?'

'I did, Jim. I asked her about her latest boyfriend.'

'Well?'

'She said she hadn't got one at the moment.'

I decided they'd gone far enough with that conversation, so I walked into the kitchen, kicked Albert out of the way, and volunteered to wash up.

'Don't be peevish with that cat,' Mother said.

I apologised to Albert, and then began to worry that I'd gone too far. Nobody apologises to Albert. Not unless they're up to something. Mother was looking at me suspiciously.

'Now then young lady, what are you after?'

I handled it well. First I said I didn't want anything, then I grinned and said:

'Lend us a few bob, Mam.'

'Ask your father,' she said, and everything went back to normal.

It had been a near thing. I left it till lunchtime then, for safety's sake.

I was drying the dishes.

'Mam,' I said, 'What does "elope" mean?'

'Why do you want to know that?'

'Oh, it doesn't matter,' I said, hastily.

I chattered on and on, but I knew she wasn't listening. Then, I shot upstairs. Maddy was drying her hair. I'd left the back of my English book open, and I continued where I'd left off before lunch.

'They all begin with EL and I've to put them in a sentence,' I said to Maddy – not that she particularly wanted to know.

'Go fetch Mam's heated rollers,' she said.

'Yes madam, straight away madam, three bags full madam,' I said, snootily, but I went for them all the same.

'Anything else madam?' I asked, when I

got back.

But sarcasm is lost on Maddy.

'No thanks,' she said.

I settled down at the table again with my books.

'Elegant. Elipse. Elusive. Elevate. Electrocute . . .' I mumbled to myself.

I carried on pretending to work until I heard Mam's feet on the stairs.

'Maddy, what does "elope" mean?'

She started to explain. I leaned forward, so that unconsciously she raised her voice.

'. . . well, when a boy and a girl love each other, and their parents are unreasonable, and they run away to get married . . .'

'Does it have to be kept a secret?' I asked, quite loudly.

'Oh, a big secret,' Maddy said, 'Or there's no point in it . . .'

I heard my mother's step retreating down the stair, and I smiled to myself.

Now it was only a matter of time.

We'd all had tea. Dad and Mother were watching telly, and Maddy was upstairs dolling herself up to go out with Sarah. I'd reckoned on the action starting around five thirty, but it was nearly six o'clock already. Not that it made any difference to the plan, but I was getting nervous.

I sat on the front step keeping watch and talking to Albert — at a safe distance. Then at last I saw Malcolm coming down the street. I nearly had second thoughts when I saw him pushing his bike with the window cleaning gear.

'You can leave your bike in the shed,' I said, kicking Albert out of the way.

I didn't want him scaring Malcolm off.

'Just the front will do,' I said, looking round to make sure nobody else had seen him arrive. 'Where do you want to start?'

'Where's Maddy?' he said.

'Up there. That's our room.'

'That's as good a place as any,' he said.

He didn't know it, but he'd just cooked his goose.

'Tell you what,' I said, 'I'll fill your bucket with water from the bathroom, and hand it out to you through the window.'

I trotted off with his bucket and cloths, while he played with the ladder. I left the bucket at the back door, though, and wandered through the house to the living room. I'd planned to say, 'He's making quite a racket of it out there isn't he?' and to disappear before they could ask me any ques-

75

tions. But I didn't need to do anything. He was making such a commotion with his ladder that they were already looking out of the window. My mother was whispering.

'Oh Jim, what are you going to do about it? Jim you must do something about it. Keep calm Jim . . .'

Dad just looked. They didn't need me to stir it, they were doing quite nicely by themselves.

I went out to the back again. Albert hadn't wasted any time. He'd found a new den among the cloths in Malcolm's bucket — all smelly and damp.

'Hello, you soggy moggy,' I said. 'You're catching on fast.'

Meanwhile, Dad had gone out the front way. I crept round the back, and round the outside of the house to the side wall. I leaned against the brickwork to listen. The whole thing was a riot, but I'd arrived just in time for the punchline.

Dad was standing at the bottom of the ladder, and in heavy sarcastic tones he said:

'While you're up there boy, you might as well clean the windows!'

'I would, sir,' Malcolm said, 'if I'd got a bucket.'

I turned up eventually with his bucket, playing it all innocent and blaming Albert. I was a bit peeved that they took me at face value. But you should have heard Dad and Mam tearing into Maddy after Malcolm had gone. It was great.

Mrs Etherington

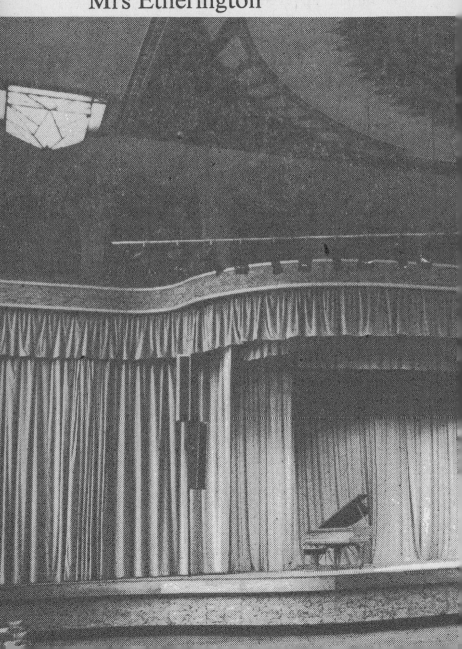

Mrs Etherington

I've always tried to do the best for my children. God knows I've only wanted what's good for them. It's only natural. I wanted them to have a better chance than we did. When I think of all the sacrifices we've made. Ungrateful, that's what it is. When I think of how we've scraped and saved.

And our Joan turning like that.

The things she said.

'I didn't ask to be born,' she said.

As if anybody does!

I'd never have spoken to my mother like that. I'd have known what for if I did! And when Dad came home, he'd have had the belt out. But Jack's too soft with her. It's with her being the youngest. And the gap between her and the other two.

She's been more trouble than the other two put together. Not like our Sue. Never a day's trouble with her. Never a moment's worry.

With a good husband and a lovely baby. The spitting image of her mum. And our Michael . . . he was a real lad. Never out of mischief.

I miss having him at home. And Canada seems such a long way away. But he never forgets his old mum. They do some lovely cards in Canada. With such nice verses on them. And always a big present at Christmas. He's getting on well, our Michael. Doing well for himself. So proud of him we are.

'A chip off the old block,' Dad says.

But our Joan!

It's enough to turn my hair grey. Having a girl nowadays is such a responsibility. It's that television that does it. I keep saying I've a good mind to send it back. And that school isn't much better. Giving her ideas. And some of those teachers look like they could do with a good wash!

Things were a lot different when I was at school. You learnt your Ps and Qs then.

And that's another thing. Fancy saying that! And in front of Granny Etherington, as well. Disgusting!

It's not as if I'm old fashioned. I like pop music. But they play it loud enough to burst your eardrums. And that exhibitionism. And all the silly screaming at concerts.

I'm not narrow-minded. It's not as if we're strict. We try to be reasonable. I mean, you can't have brought three children into the world without knowing a bit about ... er ... sex. But there are limits. Wait till she's got children of her own.

And that's another thing. I don't want her bringing trouble on us. She's too young to know her own mind. Too young to be going steady.

'Whatever would the neighbours think?' she says, in that mocking voice of hers.

Now that's not fair of her. I've never talked like that in my life. We've got very nice neighbours. Mrs H is a real lady. You wouldn't catch her coming in at all hours!

They all just want their own way. With never a by-your-leave. Wants a telephone now, she does. She thinks money grows on trees. And I've not had a holiday in years.

Her clothes cost the earth. And all that warpaint! Purple eyeshadow, I ask you. She looks like she's been in a fight. They don't know when they're well off.

If our Joan's not careful, people will think she's no good. They'll think she's a tart. She'll get a bad name.

And she's always giving lip.

'Stop your moaning,' she says.

But, I wouldn't be doing my duty by her, if I didn't tell her.

'Mind you're not back late,' I tell her.

'Boys only want one thing,' I tell her.

'They'll leave you if they get it,' I tell her.

I work every hour God sends. God knows I've tried my best. I don't know what things are coming to!

It makes my blood boil when I think of some of the things she's said. And I get so worried for her when I think of what she might be up to. You can't tell me they're up to any good. Out all hours.

And those boys she goes with. Trousers so tight they can't sit down.

And all that other stuff they wear. They look like they've enlisted in somebody's army. And their hair! It's too short or too long. And if it's in between, they can't leave it alone. Yellow streaks. Fancy cuts. They're like nancy boys. Some of them even have perms, and wear curlers. They look like Shirley Temple. And I'd swear to it that they wear perfume.

They've more money than sense. Men were men, when I was her age.

In fact, when I was her age . . . when I was her age . . . when I was her age . . . Yes. When I was her age it was the first time I'd ever been kissed.

The summers seemed to be long in those days, and life was full of promise. I don't know if that was because it was the years after the war, or just because we were young. Those days come to me in brightly coloured memories, even though I know our streets up north were grey and drab.

Perhaps everybody looks back at the years of their youth, and thinks things were better then. We weren't better off for money. Far from it. But we got fun out of making do. You could get a laugh out of painting a line down the back of your legs, or rubbing in cocoa to pretend you were wearing stockings. Even when you could afford stockings, it was only a job lot from the market – a bag of rejects. You knew the dye would run, or one leg would be six foot long. Once I got a pair with no feet at all!

I can see us now, my pal Mavis and me, our hair in turbans, chattering over the clatter of our court shoes on the cobbles. We thought we were the bee's knees and the cat's whiskers. It would be Saturday afternoon and we'd be coming back down the alleyway from the market.

To hear us, you'd have thought we'd had such adventures. And all we'd done would be to laugh at some fat lady behind a stall, and gollop a hot black pudding. We might have bought a thing or two: a fancy button from the button counter, or a bit of slab cake for tea.

I always had tea at their house on Saturdays. Then we'd go to the nine-penny pictures at the Roxy. But I remember one night, one special night. The night we went to our first dance.

My mother would have had a fit if she'd known. She thought the Palais de Dance was a den of iniquity, and that painted ladies went there. I liked the sound of painted ladies.

Ma wasn't all that happy about the pictures, either. She said they gave girls Ideas. She only gave in about me going there on Saturdays, because she thought we took Mavis's granny along, and were therefore doing a kindness.

Mavis's granny was a proper card. She

liked her glass of stout.

'It puts iron in me blood,' she used to say, 'and at my age, having thin blood does you no good, no good at all.'

The amount she drank, she must have had more iron than blood.

We used to drop her off at an old spit and sawdust pub, the Duke of York, and pick her up on the way back. We'd tell her the plot of the film, but tone it down in case she got over-excited. Mavis's battling granny, doing the Arrival of the Cavalry or Fred Astaire and Ginger Rogers, had to be seen to be believed.

Usually, I left them at the corner of their street — unless Granny was being impossible. In that case, I'd give Mavis a hand.

The routine was to get Granny straight up the stairs to bed. She called them 'The jolly old dancers'. The stairs led straight up from the front door, and Granny at her most excited was more than a match for the pair of us. We'd make one heck of a commotion going up those stairs. Mavis's mam used to shout up:

'If it taxes you that much you shouldn't go to the pictures so often.'

Granny would scream back:

'You're always trying to deny me my bit of pleasure. Any road, pictures aren't what they were. Where's Fatty Arbuckle, that's what I'd like to know?'

Looking back at it, I realise it was some sort of family game. Mavis's mother wasn't fooled for one minute — you could smell the drink a mile off.

I liked Mavis's mother.

She was a widow, and my mother used to say:

'I don't know how she manages without a man behind her. Still, they don't seem to go short.'

And I can remember, in all innocence, explaining that they had a lot of uncles in their family.

Back then, I worked in the weaving shed, and Mavis worked in the winding shop. That meant Mavis earned less than me. But she did better than me for money in her purse, because she didn't put anything in the house-keeping tin, and I had to turn all mine over, rain or shine. My mother said Mavis was spoilt.

'Mark my words, her mother'll rue the day.'

I soon learnt that the less said about Mavis

and her mother, the better. So I never told my mother how Mavis's mother taught us to put on make-up. Well, you can imagine what would've happened. I only once went into our house wearing lipstick, and it was like a red rag to a bull.

'You can wipe that muck off your face. You look like a trollop. Reminds me of a circus clown.'

So I kept my little collection of Ponds and Betty Lou at Mavis's house,. And my clip-on ear-rings.

Anyway, the Saturday I'm thinking of, we made a special effort to look nice. I can laugh at it now, but we took it deadly serious at the time. I can see Mavis sticking her chewing gum on the mirror while she plastered on her lipstick. She'd a large mouth, and all that blood red made her look as if a good third of her face was mouth. But, it was the fashion. Everybody looked like they'd been eating strawberry jam or had a really nasty accident.

I suppose my mother was right. We looked dreadful. We were trying to look older I suppose, though I'm not sure why. We thought we looked so sophisticated, but when I look at old photos, we just looked middle-aged. Middle-aged teenagers! My goodness we did look a sight!

Mavis had lovely hair, though. Sleek, smooth, and blonde. It looked ever so smart wound round a stocking top to make an angel roll. I was trying to train my hair into a pageboy, with a bit of help from pipe cleaners and curling pins. It's the sort of style that needs all your hair to have the same idea. I always had trouble with the left side, and that night it was anchored by two crossed hair pins.

Both pins were sticking in my neck as we set off. With one hand I was playing with my hairpins, and with the other arm I was supporting Granny. With me at one side and Mavis at the other, it's a wonder Granny's feet ever touched the ground.

Those light nights were enchanting, but never as that one was. That night of our first dance. Even as we dropped Granny off at the Duke of York, I knew that it was no ordinary night. Nothing could dull that feeling. The length of our skirts made them flap like witches' clothes, but to me the rustle sounded like somebody whispering promises.

Mavis was in charge of the expedition, which was just as well, because I got flustered in new places. I hardly dared to look up as we arrived, being sure that everyone was staring at us. I wondered if the neck of my blouse was too low. That blouse was shell-pink silk, and quite pretty really, but I usually wore it with a brooch at the neck.

My Auntie Nellie had given me the blouse. We didn't think anything of wearing cast-offs in those days, what with clothing coupons being the way they were.

To this day I can still remember the colours of the lino at the entrance of the Palais de Dance, the carpet runner on the stairs, and the pattern of the wooden parquet floor of the dance hall. It was considered to be a posh place from when the town had seen better days, but I sensed, rather than saw, its shabby splendour.

I looked again at the neck of my blouse, and wished I'd brought my brooch. Then a sense of bravado caught me. I took a deep breath and, not having much up front, felt really pleased to see the silk swell out, as I thought, provocatively. I strutted across the dance floor behind Mavis, and though I raised my head, my glassy, tranced eyes saw nothing but the glow of the candelabras.

We sat bathed in more yellow light by a potted plant in a carpeted alcove, and arranged ourselves on a plush covered bench.

Holding my breath didn't work when I was sitting down – the silk blouse pouched forward. So I clutched at the neck, and lost all of my confidence. We'd brought our cardigans, so I put mine on, and buttoned it to the top.

'You won't be cold when we start dancing,' Mavis said.

She stood up and walked a few steps, then turned to wait for me. It wasn't a bit like dancing together at the mill in our dinner time. We kept walking all over each other's feet.

'You lead,' Mavis hissed, pulling me in the direction she wanted to go. We managed a few dances, more by good luck than good mangement.

'Stop looking at your feet,' she said. 'You're supposed to look up and smile.'

'If one of us doesn't watch our feet,' I said, 'We'll both go flying.'

We tried a clumsy twirl as the orchestra finished its medley on a flourish. The dancers clapped, looked at the band expectantly, and waited for the next number.

'Let's sit at the side,' Mavis said.

I knew she meant, 'Let's try our chances', so I nodded, and followed her across the floor again. I puffed out my chest once more, but decided there wasn't much point with a buttoned-up cardigan.

I breathed out again.

'What are you sighing for?' Mavis asked.

'Nothing,' I said, and sat down again.

The uncertainty as I stared at my feet, and waited to be asked to dance. The realisation that they wouldn't ask, unless I looked up and looked willing. The disappointment at the bald-headed, fat, little man with his tiny feet, and his pointed shiny shoes. He had to ask me twice before I remembered to answer him. The disappointment — but also the pleasure — of knowing that someone at least wanted me.

Most of the dancing was proper ballroom stuff, and this was a quickstep. I always danced the man's part when I danced with Mavis, but after treading on the fat man's shiny shoes, I remembered to go backwards. I looked back at Mavis over my shoulder. The arching of her plucked eyebrow conveyed a clear message. Bald-headed men didn't count.

The little man was a good dancer. He steered me efficiently, and I felt like a clockwork doll. It was accomplished exhibition stuff, but not a bit sentimental.

Then the band struck up a jitterbugging

variation of the tune — there were still a few Americans around in those days. My mother had warned me about them. But Mavis and I weren't likely to get a look in. They'd got a corner of the floor to themselves, and had been jiving all the time. Now they took over the centre, and the rest of the dancers hung around watching — or else made for the bar, particularly the local lads. They didn't take kindly to Americans, though there wasn't likely to be any trouble.

The little fat man wasn't built for jitter-bugging, and he had enough sense not to try.

'Would you and your friend like a drink?' he asked, as he escorted me back to the seat.

I had a port and lemon, and felt wicked. It was lovely.

Mavis danced with the fat man next. It was a slow foxtrot. She coped very well, and from the smirk on her face as she passed me, I realised that this time round, fat men counted.

After a second port and lemon, the fat man excused himself and left us. I was getting hot, and I unbuttoned my cardigan. Suddenly, I became aware that Mavis was talking to somebody.

'You've a cheek,' she said.

Two boys were standing a few feet away

from us. One was chewing gum and smiling. Mavis turned to me, but managed to give him the eye at the same time.

'He says, "Can he walk me home?" Got a cheek, hasn't he?'

She did the sidelong-eyebrow-raised look at him.

'Aren't we supposed to have a few dances first?' she asked.

'I can't dance,' he grinned.

I opened my mouth, but didn't say anything. It wasn't true that he couldn't dance. I'd passed him on the floor when he was dancing with a redhead. She was over with the Americans now, I noticed.

'I was thinking of having another port and lemon first,' Mavis hinted.

I went pink with embarrassment.

'You can have lemonade and like it,' he grinned.

The other boy smiled at me.

'She won't bite,' Mavis said to him, and got up to follow her lad to the bar.

'That's a nice blouse,' the other boy said, shyly.

That encouraged me to undo the rest of the cardigan buttons. We set off across the edge of the dance floor. I took a deep breath again.

'Ping!' went the top button of my blouse.

Hurriedly, I fastened up my cardigan, and whispered to Mavis about safety pins.

'It looks all right without a top button,' she said.

'It's not decent,' I whispered back. 'If my mother saw it without a brooch even, she'd make me wear a bib.'

'It's not as if there's anything to see,' Mavis's bloke laughed, and to my horror I realised he'd heard every word.

I went off to the Ladies armed with a safety pin. There were lots of girls touching up their make-up, checking the seams of their stockings, and hitching up suspenders. There were no glamorous Painted Ladies, but all the same, I felt inexperienced and shabby. I was amazed at the coarseness of their language. Harsh swear words hung on the powder-filled air.

I looked in the mirror. The two hairpins were straggling out at right angles, my eye make-up had run, and my nose was shiny. I smeared away a smut from my cheek, then realised it had once been my pencilled beauty spot. There was no point trying to patch up my face. I'd have to remove my war paint before I got home, anyway. I washed it off as best I could and combed my hair.

I fished in my clutch bag for my little bottle of Californian Poppy, and put a discreet dab behind my ears and on my wrists. Then, I had second thoughts and applied another dab. In my nervousness the bottle tipped. I returned to the hall reeking of the cheap scent.

And then panic.

Mavis wasn't there. Nor were the two boys. I hadn't been that long, surely. Anyway, the drinks were still on the counter. No, definitely no sign of Mavis, but there was quite a commotion going on in the doorway that led outside. I saw the back of an angel roll hairdo in the middle of a tangle of arms. Then a shriek — and I knew it just had to be Mavis. She sounded like her granny when she screamed.

I pushed my way through the gathering crowd, and there were Mavis and the red-headed girl trying to tug each other's hair out by the roots.

'Stop it! Stop it!' I demanded of a man next to me.

'Not flaming likely,' he said. 'I don't fancy committing suicide. Needs a lion-tamer to stop that pair.'

I ploughed into the middle, and tried to

catch hold of the redhead. A real talon of a finger nail caught in my blouse, and I heard a rip and the pinging of another button. That did it. I got really angry then.

'Go to it girls,' some bloke was shouting, but I didn't need any encouragement.

Nor did the redhead's friends. Nor a guy nearby who turned on the bloke nearest him, and popped him in the eye. The one on the receiving end of the punch fell back, but the pressure of the crowd pushed him forward again, and he fell flat on his face. There was a lot of falling about, and pushing and shoving, but it wasn't a bit like you see on the pictures. It was just an untidy muddle, more like a confused dance than a fight.

It didn't take the management long to get us under control, and they were rougher than any of us had been.

So there we were, on the pavement outside. Mavis with her angel roll half hanging over one ear, and looking not at all angelic, and me buttoning my cardigan to hide my torn blouse. Under a distant gaslight we could see the redhead linking Mavis's bloke, and staggering up the street.

My lad was still with us. I hadn't seen him in the fight, but his clothes looked like somebody had been sweeping the floor with him, and one ear was pink and swollen.

'Which way?' he asked.

'Along here,' I said, and, linking Mavis, I set off. He tagged along.

'This right for the bus station?' he asked.

'Yes.'

'I'll walk you,' he said.

I'd always imagined a more romantic setting for such an offer. Mavis was trying to tuck in her angel roll, and swore under her breath. Surprisingly, she wasn't very much the worse for wear. It was mostly her dignity that was hurt.

'She was a street walker, if ever I saw one,' she said.

'He's engaged to her,' the boy volunteered.

'He's welcome,' Mavis said.

'They deserve each other,' I added, clutching Mavis's arm more firmly.

We walked along in silence. There was something uneven about the way he was moving. Looking out of the corner of my eye, I realised that he was playing at walking along the pavement without standing on any of the cracks between the flag stones. For a moment he was quite oblivious of us, lost in his little game. Then he became aware of me watching. He laughed nervously and chanted:

> *'If you stand on a nick*
> *You'll marry a brick.'*

I smiled, but he started walking properly, though the rhythm of normal steps seemed to escape him for a while. I think that's when I first thought that he was rather sweet.

There was a chip shop on the next corner, and he bought a bag of chips and a bottle of dandelion and burdock to share between the three of us. We sat on a wall outside, and I got a better look at him. He was nothing special, and his hair looked like it had been cut with a knife and fork, especially one spiky piece at the front.

Usually if we met any lads, Mavis button-holed the conversation. She meant to be flirtatious, but it just came over as loud. But that night, she was still smarting from the redhead incident, and couldn't be bothered to be charming. It was up to me to keep the conversation going. I fixed his spike of hair with a steely stare, and besieged him with questions. It was like the Inquisition.

He was called Tom, he worked at a colliery, and he lived in the next town. He had five younger brothers, one older sister, and two cats. I suppose he had a mother and father, too, but I didn't like to ask that. He liked his brothers, he liked his sister and he didn't mind cats. He liked his job, his town, our town, but he didn't think much of the Palais. He hadn't read any good books lately, and he'd never been to the Roxy. Yes, he liked chips. He liked tripe, and his sister was partial to black puddings. He didn't reckon much to black puddings himself.

We bought another helping of chips, smiled at each other in the steamy mirror, and continued on our way. Mavis was getting as sour as last week's milk.

We were nearly at our corner when it dawned on us.

'Heck!' Mavis said. 'We forgot Granny!'

I offered to go back with her, but she wasn't being very friendly. So Tom and I carried on.

We didn't have much to say to each other, and I'd run out of questions. There was another chip shop by the canal and its reflection lit the dismal water. In the shop, there was a handwritten notice in copperplate writing:

Fish and chips are good for you,
And here you get the best.

100

A little salt and vinegar,
And they are easy to digest.

Tom and I looked at it. Then he turned to me.

'I like poetry,' he said.

Sitting on the bank of the Cut, we shared a fish and half-pennorth of bits. It was very companionable being there together, but the atmosphere faded with the last crispy bit of batter. I felt embarrassed sitting so close to a stranger, and I made to move, but he was already scrambling to his feet.

He threw the newspaper, and caught it with boyish kicks till it plopped to rot among the prams and rubbish in the murky waters of the canal.

We continued walking.

'In case you're wondering,' he said. 'I'm not going to try and kiss you goodnight.'

I didn't know whether to be glad or disappointed.

'That's fine by me,' I said. 'I'd hit you with my clutch bag if you did.'

It's embarrassing to remember that part of the conversation. He eyed me nervously. I moved my clutch bag to the hand furthest from him, just in case he took me literally.

He wasn't the first boy I'd ever walked with

down the street, but in one way he *was* the first. All the others had been at school with me, or were neighbours from down our way. We'd seen each other grow up, and we still saw, peering through the growing up, the faces as we'd known them in childhood. I'd fancied some of them, too. But never let on.

But this boy had appeared with no past, no familiar things to laugh about. I didn't know where to start.

Suddenly, I felt his hand brush mine. It had been accidental.

'Sorry,' we both said, and I wondered if the contact had shot up his arm like it had done mine.

I was conscious of my free arm, almost as if I'd one arm too many. I managed to will it to move up, and I held my bag with both hands. That seemed even more awkward, so I let one hand swing free again.

I could sense he was looking at me, but I stared earnestly at the houses we were passing. There was a woman sitting in a front window, and I'd looked full into her room before I realised.

'Nosey young madam,' she yelled. 'Get yer eyeful, did yer?'

Embarrassed, I turned my head towards

Tom. He smiled nervously. I don't think he'd noticed the woman. I stared straight ahead, and tried to get my legs to walk and my hips to swing. I sensed he was looking at my hand.

Then, his hand shot out and grabbed mine. I realised he was as nervous as I was, because he was staring ahead, and his face was fixed rigid.

'He's a fast mover,' I said to myself, taking pleasure in the thought even though I knew it wasn't true.

It was that port and lemon feeling again. I savoured it for a moment. I wondered what I ought to do about it. I didn't want him to think it was the first time I'd held hands, either. We walked along in silence, as if the two clasping hands didn't belong to either of us.

I was terrified that someone who knew my mother might see us. And as for Ma herself! The thought didn't bear thinking. She'd've come right across and boxed my ears. And what if she was out in the street waiting for me? She'd never been before, but there was always a first time.

'This way,' I said, the words falling like pebbles on a pond of silence.

I pulled him right instead of left at the

crossroads. I'd too many conflicting emotions to be able to converse as well, but it didn't strike me till later, that he'd had nothing to say for himself, either. I was busy justifying in my head why I couldn't let him see our street. I couldn't risk Mam being out with the hatchet. Or was there more than that? I've often wondered. Not that there was anything to be ashamed of about Red Lion Street. But now I was seeing the whole district through the eyes of a stranger. I paused, half thinking of turning back towards home. We were outside the entrance to a big house.

'I'll leave you here,' I muttered.

I don't know if I meant to pretend that I lived there, but that's the way it came out. I looked down at our hands, and he let go as if I'd burnt him. Then he cleared his throat noisily and blurted out a few words.

'Er, I know I said I . . . well I was thinking . . . I . . . er . . . goodnight.'

He grabbed my shoulders, and his mouth blundered against my face. For a moment, I was All Women Of All Time. As I put my hand to each side of his face and drew his head towards me, there were strange churnings in my stomach. I kissed him. Then, pretending to go up the drive of the big house, I hid in the bushes till he'd gone.

Sometimes I wonder if I actually remember the moment — or if I only remember the remembering.

I thought about it often, later. I'd felt so mature one minute, and the next, like a kid, skipping, jumping, dancing on air, playing hide and seek . . . everything that kids do.

We didn't arrange to see each other again. I don't know if we wanted to. I didn't realise we hadn't. It never crossed my mind.

'What a forward young man,' I kept saying, as I walked home, building the memory into a dream.

In fact, I never met a man who was really forward until I met Jack. And I married him!

But, that night ended as I had dreaded, with my mother standing at the end of the street. It boded ill, and I registered the omens. Scarf and raincoat with her slippers on.

'Where've you been, you slut? Murdered to death I've been with worry,' she said.

My brain wasn't working logically, and somehow I thought she knew it all. I didn't even question why she was at the corner.

'Written all over your face it is,' she said.

But I never found out what was written there.

I can laugh about it now, but it was all Mavis's granny's fault. We'd left her that bit too long, and the extra half hour saw her really sloshed. Granny had hit someone with a bottle. In fact, she'd laid out three of them, before a bobby got her under control. The story had spread like wildfire. And reached home before I did. I know my mother thought I was a real tramp, a proper Painted Lady.

She had a nice turn of phrase, too, when it came to lecturing on The Evils Of Demon Drink. And every phrase was punctuated with a clout round the ear.

I didn't appreciate being told that the Palais was The Portal To Perdition and that Painted Ladies danced through it down The Primrose Path To The Everlasting Bonfire. I just felt empty, with her going on like that. I didn't even shiver at the thought of what my dad might do. All I felt was loneliness. All I'd wanted was to share with someone the joys of that very special evening.

As I climbed the stairs, banished to bed, and murmuring 'such a forward young man', I swore that if I ever had any children, we'd have a different relationship . . .

If I ever had any children . . .

If I ever had any children . . .

Bean

Bean

When I was little I used to have a dream — the same dream more or less. There was a war on in the dream. Blood and gore everywhere. I like a bit of blood and gore. If it wasn't a war, it would be gangsters, but it was still the same dream. There would be lots of action. Ratatat tat! Whizz! Bang! Capow! Thud! Wallop! Mutilations left, right and centre. It'd all be happening, and there I'd be in the middle.

It wasn't a dream really. It was a nightmare. There I'd be in the middle of the action, but in the corner of a bombed-out room. I'd be crouching, waiting for *them* to come and get me. Whatever the dream, I was missing all the fun. I was crouching, waiting, hiding.

Hiding at the Ice Rink, under the stairs, I remembered that dream. I got the feeling of being there before.

The stairs led from the rink up to the bar. I

heard one set of boots veer off the stairs, and come towards my hiding place. A head loomed sideways and peered under the stairs.

'That you, Bean?'

I sighed with relief. It was the voice of my mate, Dougie. He scrambled in and crouched next to me.

'Makes a good spot this for a bit of the other,' he said, craning his neck round.

Dougie was always spotting places that were good for a bit of the other. The places were all right, but he had trouble finding the girls. There were more sounds of feet from above. I grabbed Dougie's elbow. He was testing the floor for dust, for when he got a chance of a bit of the other.

'It'll be Sid. He was straight behind me. Yeah! Good spot this. Better than the Disco passage.'

Sid crept in.

'We suspected you'd be here,' he said.

'How come?' I asked.

'You got a thing about cupboards. Whenever there's any aggravation, you always shut yourself in a cupboard. There ain't no cupboards, and this was the next best thing.'

I glared at him in the darkness. Dougie

111

laughed.

'Aggravation!' he mocked. 'You swallowed a dictionary?'

'He's been like that ever since Simple Simon told him he stood a good chance of passing that English exam. Bloody great fairy,' I said.

'Shurrup,' Dougie snapped. 'We'll all get some aggravation if these bouncers catch up with us. And it's still a busted nose in any language.'

'Get the philosopher!' Sid whistled, but then we went silent, and peered between the slats of the stairs.

I smiled to myself, thinking of Sid. That one compliment from our English teacher had gone to his head. It's probably the only one he's ever had. As a result – according to Sid – nobody talked any more, they conversed. They didn't think, they reflected. They didn't walk, they perambulated. And, according to Sid, people didn't die, they expired. Maybe it was improving Sid's English, but it wasn't doing anything for ours. I've never heard Dougie swear so much in his life.

I scrambled over the other two, and risked peering out round the edge of the steps.

'Mind where you're putting those bloody bunions of yours,' Dougie grumbled, getting up, and squinting under my arm.

The red jackets were disappearing down the other end of the rink.

'Those bleeding bouncers think they're it,' Dougie continued. 'How were we to know the little kiddies hadn't finished their session? Those bouncers speed skate more than we do.'

'They don't knock people over,' I said, to be fair.

'Hey, dig that!' Sid laughed.

He'd pulled off a piece of wood to make a peephole, and he was spying out. Then he remembered his English.

'What a spectacle!' he said.

'Where?' I asked.

'See that ole geezer, perambulating round on one leg, and giving it all this.'

He half stood to waggle one leg as a demonstration, and whacked his head on the steps.

We laughed and set off up to try the bar. It wasn't our lucky night.

'Three pints of beer,' I said, being the tallest.

'How old?'

'Draught, not bottled.'

'You, sunshine. Not the flaming bitter. Do I

have to spell it out to you? How old are you?'

'Eighteen,' I lied.

He didn't say anything. He just looked, and folded his arms.

'Yesterday,' I said. 'My birthday was yesterday. You'd think it was a rotten police state.'

'What year?'

'Er . . . now?'

'Born. What year were you born, Dewdrop?'

'Nineteeen . . . er . . .' I stammered, licking my lips and wishing my maths was up to it.

'Out.'

'Forty-nine.' Sid said, over my shoulder, just as Dougie said 'fifty-nine' over the other shoulder.

'I said OUT. And take Slack Alice and Apricot Lil with yer!'

'Fifty-eight?' Dougie offered.

'Listen wise guys. Get your arses out of 'ere. Now!'

''E don't spare no language, does 'e?' Sid said. 'It's a good job we're not children!'

We ran.

Back under the stairs, we peered out again.

'Their beer's bloody dear, anyway,' Dougie

muttered.

'Extortionate,' Sid agreed.

'We can get one in across the road before we go home, anyway,' I said.

'Do you think it's safe back on the ice?' Dougie asked.

'Why not?' I said. 'Big Mo's just come in. That'll keep 'em occupied.'

'Dig mush,' Sid said, and muttered 'occupied' to himself all the way back to the ice.

We skated.

'It's bloody cold when you hang around here,' Dougie grumbled. 'Let's put a spurt on.'

'Go easy,' I said, tagging on to his arm to slow him down.

Big Mo skated up to us. She took it that we were waiting for her. The bells tinkled on her toecaps. She was proud of her new skates. Ours were hired. National Health boots. But we didn't make any cracks about hers. You never knew how Mo would take things. She wasn't called Big Mo for nothing.

'Coming round?' she asked, and grabbed hold of my arm.

The others linked on to me, and we formed a chain. A whistle went across the other end of the rink where a group of kiddies were falling about. One of them, from our school, skated over and joined us. He linked on to the other side of Mo.

'Ger off, Leroy,' she said. 'I wanna lead.'

He speeded up to the other end of our chain, and did a sudden stop by Sid so that the ice sprayed all over the place. I looked round warily for the bouncers, but the nearest one was among the wooden chairs. He was collecting bags from under the seats. They're bomb precaution mad nowadays. He turned his head slightly, and I saw that he was the guy we'd had the first barney with.

'Don't hang about,' I said to Mo. 'Let's get a move on.'

'Who d'yer think you are, Big-mouth? If you don't watch it I'll thump you,' she said, but she was smiling.

More kids from our school had arrived, and Leroy whistled them over. The longer the chain the more Mo was pleased. She hung on to wait for them to sort themselves out, and I kept a wary eye on the bouncer. His sort have long memories. Stupid elephant.

I glanced back down the line. That's when I first noticed Sal had joined us. I smiled down the chain at her, just as Mo muttered in my ear.

'I 'ates that kiddie there. That Sallie

Pearce.'

I was watching Sal. She was getting to be quite something, lately.

Growing up, she was. All over. I'd known her since the Infants but I was beginning to wonder where she'd been all my life.

Mo started off suddenly. I wasn't expecting it, and nearly fell flat on my face. We gained speed, and gradually our caterpillar sorted itself out. More kids tagged on, and after the third circuit, Mo started on a figure of eight.

'Get stuck in,' she yelled, as our chain narrowed the curve to cut across its own tail. We were going well, but my heart was up in my throat, because I knew that Mo wouldn't be satisfied till we got in a muddle, and ended in a pile up. You couldn't hear much of the disc jockey normally, and what you could hear you couldn't understand, but he didn't have a chance now everyone was screaming and yelling.

The pile-up came sooner than I'd expected, and Dougie's arm was jerked from mine. Mo and I were caught in the thrust of our own momentum, and off we shot out of control. The 'No Smoking' sign flashed by on wings, and smack. We hit the crash barrier. Whistles were blowing from all areas. Out of the corner of my eye, I saw our bouncer hurdling the seats to get back to the rink.

I picked myself up, and tried to give a hand to Mo. She pushed me away, but she was smiling again.

'Bulldog next,' she grinned.

I laughed to myself. She always played Bulldog even if nobody else was playing.

The bouncers sorted out the tangle of arms and legs, and then they tried a bit of psychology. The lights began to signal that the next session was pairs. That was one of the specials for Wednesday nights: Lights out — kiss your partner.

I saw Dougie scrambling up to find himself a bird. I laughed, and skated over to him. Mo followed. Dougie grabbed my arm, and manoeuvred me through the crowd to a space.

'What's Mo following for?' he demanded, in a panic. 'You don't think she fancies me, do yer?'

'You could do worse,' Sid said, joining us. 'She's not a bad kid.'

'Not bloody likely,' Dougie said. 'Remember that Terry whatsit. Fancied 'im she did. Split 'is head open at the swimmin' baths, she did. He still likes 'er an' all. Effin' masochist!'

'That's a big word,' Sid said, in admiration.

'Who you going round with, Bean?'

'Nobody,' I said.

'I'm getting shut,' Dougie said, and hurtled away off the rink.

'I bags Sallie Pearce,' I said.

Mo skated up.

''E's gone thataway,' Sid said.

'Who?'

'Andy. Dougie. You know. Fancies you summat rotten 'e does.'

All three of us are called Andy. That's why we're Sid, Bean and Dougie. Mo looked at me. I didn't want to land Dougie in it any further so I just smiled.

'Don't hang about,' Sid said, grabbing my arm and towing me off. He dropped me off by Sallie Pearce. She smiled, and I caught hold of her hand. I took her once round.

We were just starting on the second lap when the lights went out. Some girl near me was growling, 'Ger off,' and somebody else was shouting, 'Get stuck in,' but Sal and I were too busy to say anything. Then, lights up. I reckoned they'd make us go round about ten times before the next session. Rotten kill-joys.

Dougie had managed to get a bird, but she

wasn't much cop. As we passed them I heard him say:

'I know a nice place. Not too dusty.'

She didn't take him up on it. Next time round he was skating by himself.

I stuck my tongue out, and he gave us an 'up-yours' sign.

People began to link up, so I grabbed Dougie as he whizzed past the next time, and he grabbed Sid. Mo tagged on the other end of Leroy, but they were facing in the opposite direction. There was nothing for it but to let the line spin in the centre of the rink. It just had to be another pile-up. We were on the verge of it, as the lights went out. I felt Sal's hand tug away from mine as she tried to save herself. There was no time for kissing this round. It was all I could do to stop myself kissing the ice.

We were out of the tangle as the lights went up. Mo was between Sal and me, and there was a red raw gash along the back of Sal's hand. It took me a minute to take it in that she'd had an accident. She turned on Mo.

'You bitch,' she said. 'You did that deliberately.'

'Says who?' Mo sneered. 'You?'

'Yes, me,' answered Sal, as cold as the ice.

A bouncer arrived before everything turned nasty. He took Sal off to the First Aid in the office. Mo took that as a surrender.

'Good riddance to bad rubbish,' she said.

Then she tried to link me.

'Come on round,' she said.

'Sod off,' I told her.

The other bouncers were speeding over, and among them were the ones we'd upset earlier.

'Let's make ourselves scarce,' Sid said, but already a beefy hand was on his shoulder.

'What's your name?'

'Andy.'

'And yours?'

'Andy.'

'Oh yeah. What about you, wise guy?'

'Mine's Andy, too,' I said.

'Three wise monkeys eh? Well this ain't no zoo.'

'Oh yeah?'

Well that was the end of the skating for us. As Sid said, it wasn't one of those conversations one should endeavour to pursue.

In the pub across the way, he mentioned Mo.

'Hey, d'yer think Mo did do that deliberate like, to Sal?'

'Dunno,' I said, 'I've noticed her picking on Sal a lot in class, just lately.'

'She's like that to everybody.'

I didn't argue the toss, because I wasn't sure of my ground. I'd only noticed Mo getting at Sal, because I'd started watching Sal more lately. Whether they'd always been like that, I couldn't remember, and I hadn't given much thought to Mo's treatment of everyone else – apart from the obvious things like the black eyes and the busted noses.

As we got off the bus, we saw Mo was hanging around the stop.

'Where did you lot get to?' she demanded.

'Stopped off for a pint,' Sid said.

'Got a fag?'

'No. It's football season.'

'Bleedin' sportsmen!' she said.

As we walked along, she brought out a set of pictures from the photo machine.

'Rogues' Gallery,' Dougie said.

'Watch yer 'ealth, you.'

'They're not bad,' I said. 'Whose is that hand sticking in front of the camera?'

'Just some kid,' she said. 'Next time I'll chop it off.'

'Was Sallie Pearce all right?' Sid asked.

'Dunno. Stupid cat!'

I was going to say something about it myself but she carried on.

'Anybody babysitting tonight?'

'No,' Dougie laughed. 'I never sit on babies!'

She swung her skates at him, and the light glinted on the blades.

'You ought to get some guards for them,' I said.

'Bodyguards or lifeguards?' Dougie asked, safely behind a hedge.

'If you're having one of your funny turns,' I said, 'I'm going home.'

Mo tagged on because she goes the same way. As we passed the library she pointed out her name carved in the wood. 'Mo rules OK.'

'Wherever you go round 'ere, you can see my name,' she said, proudly.

On the Supermarket wall, it was in silver spray nicked from the Art room.

'One day it'll be written in blood,' she boasted.

As we came round the corner where she lived, she handed me the photos.

'You can have these if you want,' she said.

Next day, Sal came to school with her hand in a bandage. At break, I asked her if she'd go out with me.

'I'll think about it. Tell you this afto,' she said.

But I knew the answer was yes.

Mo was in a filthy mood all day. When we came together for English last lesson, it was obvious there'd been trouble in the Domestic Science option. There was meringue in everybody's hair.

That night, Sal was babysitting for her mum and dad. I hung around outside. On the fourth time round the block, I nearly ran into Mo taking some empty bottles back. I slid out of sight and waited. Sal's grandad set off to the Legion, and soon afterwards, her parents came down to the bus stop arm in arm. I looked up for the signal. Front bedroom light on and curtain half closed. The coast was clear.

She let me in, and kissed me. Off to a good start. Then she brewed some coffee. We turned the telly low, and snuggled down on the floor, leaning against the settee. This is the life, I thought.

'Our coffee's gone cold,' she laughed.

'Who needs coffee?' I said.

At the next lull, I whispered.

'I bet Sid would have a word for this.'

'Who needs words?' Sal replied.

'What about your whatsit?' I asked, indicating upstairs.

'It's sleeping. Do *you* go babysitting?'

'They don't let me. There were these kiddies see. Three of 'em. I let 'em stay up to see *The Curse of the Werewolf*. Had flaming nightmares they did. Cried themselves to sleep.'

She started laughing. It seemed as good a cue as any to carry on kissing. We had about an hour's peace and quiet, and then we heard somebody coming up the path.

'Heck!' she said, sitting up. 'Grandad's come back early!'

'Oh hell!' I muttered, and carried on swearing as we tried to get ourselves buttoned up and tidy. I plumped on to the settee, and stared at the TV screen, as if I'd been rooted there for the past hour. I was uncomfortably aware of my flushed cheeks.

'Don't just sit there, you idiot!' Sal squealed. 'I'm not allowed anybody in!'

There was nothing for it but a cupboard! An upstairs wardrobe. It was suffocating, and virtually soundproof. The smell of stale pipe tobacco was smothering me, and I was fighting a losing battle with a fur coat.

All sorts of thoughts were rushing through

125

my mind. Suppose I couldn't get out before her parents came home? I imagined her mother opening the door and shouting 'Rape!' I wondered if she would faint before I did!

I risked opening the door a few inches. There seemed to be a hell of a racket going on downstairs for one tottering old grandad.

'God, what's going on down there?' I thought.

It dawned on me that here was my chance. With all that noise, nobody would hear me making my getaway. I tried the window first, but it was stiff.

Bathroom, I thought, remembering it was next door. I reasoned that once I was out of the house I could go round and knock on the front door like I was visiting. After all if Grandad was going berserk, Sal would need a hand.

Quick as a flash I was in the bathroom. Up with the window. It was no problem. Leg on the sill. Look for the drainpipe. So far so good. And then I looked down. I couldn't believe it. There was Sid shinning up.

'What the hell?' we both said.

I stood back to let him clamber in. Dougie was starting up after him.

'It's Mo,' Sid said. 'She pushed her way in when Sal opened the door. We've been following her. Leroy let on that she was up to something. She's locked herself in with Sal. She's trying to bully Sal into having a babysitting party. And what are you doing here?'

'What d'yer think?'

'Crafty sod. No wonder we couldn't find you.'

'Been getting yer oar in, have yer?' Dougie asked, from halfway in over the sill.

Suddenly we heard Sal screaming my name.

'Come on!' Sid said. 'Let's go downstairs quick!'

'Hold on,' Dougie said. 'There's Mo's mates out here!'

'You what?'

'Coming up the way we did.'

It was Sid to the rescue.

'Tally ho!' he yelled, and grabbed a bucket that was below the sink.

It was full of soaking nappies.

'Bingo!' he roared, as they landed on target.

He started filling the bucket ready for the next onslaught, as Dougie and I hurtled downstairs.

We rushed into the kitchen to find Sal and Mo struggling with each other on the floor.

There was milk, eggs, sugar and coffee all over the place.

'Wow! What a mess!' Dougie whistled. 'What a mess!'

He was lost for words. I bet even Sid would have been. Dougie turned to me. I nodded.

'Yeah, I know. What a mess.'

We waded into the battle, trying to separate the two girls. Dougie picked up one unbroken egg, and squashed it on Mo's forehead. That did it. Suddenly I saw the funny side of things. I roared with laughter. Thinking about it, that ought to have made everything worse, but it didn't. When Mo saw me laughing, she stopped struggling. Then it was no effort at all to bundle Mo towards the back door. As we threw her out she yelled:

'I'm not 'aving you lot in my gang any more.'

'Is that a threat or a promise?' Dougie shouted, as we locked the kitchen door behind her.

'Some grandad,' I said to Sal.

'Lock the front door behind us, and only open it when you're sure it's us,' I said to her gently. 'We'll go and have another look round.'

Dougie and I trod eggy footmarks out

128

through the front door. Sid was at the bottom of the drainpipe by then, and there was no sign of Mo's lot.

'They gave up,' he said, laughing. 'Like the Battle of Britain it was. Up Nappy Power!'

He did a winner's lap round the garden, while Dougie and I looked at the muddy, soggy nappies strewn around our feet.

There was no sign of Mo, either – apart from the heads lopped off a few flowers. It didn't surprise me. I reckoned she'd had enough.

Back in the house, we all looked at the chaos.

'Wow! What a mess,' Dougie said.

'Your record's got stuck,' I muttered.

'Catastrophic,' Sid said. 'What an earth-quake!'

Whatever made me think he'd be stuck for words? Sal's lip was trembling. She tried to smile at Sid's comment, but it was all too much for her. She crumbled on the spot and, sitting among the broken eggshells, she burst into tears.

'Looks like she just hatched out of there,' Sid said.

That set her off crying louder than ever. We looked at each other sheepishly.

129

'Right lads,' I said. 'No mucking about. Let's get to it.'

There was no point trying to clean up, while we all looked like second-rate swill bills, so we stripped down to our underpants, and threw our clothes and shoes outside the back door.

'Leave your knickers on,' I said to Dougie.

At first we left Sal where she was on the floor, and cleaned round her. When she seemed more like herself, we told her to go upstairs, have a bath and get changed. An hour later, everything was as clean as a new pin.

'D'yer know what, Dougie?' Sid laughed, 'You'll make a good wife for somebody some day.'

Dougie didn't rise to it.

'Just look at that!' he said, proudly.

It was the carpet strip to the front door, and it looked beautiful. He'd taken off the foot marks with a damp cloth, and it looked like he'd given it an egg shampoo.

'How did you do that' I asked.

'A damp cloth, and a lot of elbow grease,' he said. 'Nothing to it, my old cock-sparrer.'

I looked round doubtfully just as Sal came downstairs.

'I dunno,' I said, 'It doesn't look right to me.'

Dougie looked round.

'It looks clean to me. Even the stuff you two did.'

'Thanks a lot,' I said.

'I know what's wrong with it,' Sid said. 'It doesn't just look clean — it looks suspiciously clean.'

'Perhaps we should mess everything up again,' Dougie suggested.

'No!' we all shouted.

Dougie's good at cleaning up, but he's even better at messing up.

'Don't worry about it,' Sal said. 'I'll just tell 'em I got bored with the telly, so I tidied up a bit, and did a few odd jobs like washing the nappies.'

'Nobody could get that bored!' Dougie said.

There was a scrabbling at the front door.

'Grandad?' I queried, looking at Sal.

'No. Mam and Dad. They've got a key!'

The key slotted into the lock, and we heard the front door open.

Talk about panic! There wasn't time to get dressed. We hurtled through the back door, and grabbed our clothes and shoes. Safely

behind the dustbins, we waited until we were
sure it was her parents and not The Enemy. I
don't know what time her grandad came
home, the dirty old stop-out!

As soon as we got the chance, we nipped
out of the yard and streaked out of sight. We
stopped round the corner, and sat on a wall to
get dressed.

'Hey,' Sid said, suddenly. 'Do you realise
what conclusion they would have come to?'
We looked at him blankly.

'What would they have thought,' he said, 'if
they'd caught us?'

I looked at him standing there all skinny
and blue in his goosepimples and underpants.

'Shurrup,' I growled.

'It's all right for you,' Dougie complained.
'You got your ration. Sid's right. I don't like
getting done for summat I never got a chance
to do.'

'Don't get on at him,' Sid said. 'He couldn't
have had much time on the job himself.'

'You're bloody right there,' I said, amazed
to find myself not exaggerating.

A knock came on a window behind us. We
were still in various stages of undress.

'Oh hell,' I said. 'Let's get a move on.'

We walked home singing:

'We're three little lambs
that have lost our way
Baa! Baa! Baa!'

I'd wondered how Mo would behave the next morning, but she didn't seem much different.

'What do you think?' I asked Sid, as we watched her.

'More truculent,' he replied, which left me no wiser.

It was English before break, and Mo was contenting herself staring at Mr Simpkin's flies. It makes him feel uncomfortable. When he writes on the blackboard, we all focus on his bald spot. That works well, too.

One of the girls got bored, and asked to go to the loo. When she came back a whisper started. I noticed some of the girls watching me. Dougie was sitting next to me, and at first he thought it was him.

'I thought they'd notice some day,' he said, flexing his muscles to pea-size.

When the looking became giggling, and I saw Sal blushing, I knew that she must have written our names in the loo. I felt quite pleased about it, and settled down to write my application letter which was the English exercise for that lesson. I looked at Simple Simon's sample letter on the board, but I couldn't read his writing so I leaned over Dougie.

'You fancy me too, ducky?' he said.

I couldn't read his writing either, so I turned round to Sid. He was applying to be a brain surgeon.

When the break bell rang, I hadn't quite finished my application to be Prime Minister. Simple Simon asked me to carry the pile of exercise books down to the staffroom. At the top of the stairs, some idiot came up behind me and gave me an almighty shove. The books went everywhere, and so did I. By the time I'd picked myself up, and counted my spare parts like my fingers and toes, I couldn't tell who it was who'd knocked me for six, but I guessed it was no accident – and I reckoned on Mo.

I didn't say anything to the others, when I joined them at the tuckshop window. Sal threw me a packet of crisps. Mo and Leroy came up. Mo was offering everybody sweets including Sal. She made a special point of offering one to me. I looked her straight in the eye, but there was no sign to tell me she'd had anything to do with the accident on the stairs. I emptied the last crumbs from the crispbag

134

on to the yard, and booted the bag at Dougie.

The pigeons were circling above as they usually did. They'd land after break, when we were all safely back in class.

I spent most of the next lesson watching the pigeons. Mo sat next to me for some reason best known to herself.

I eyed her uneasily, but she was working at being friendly. I was watching a one-legged pigeon that came every day. We called him Cassidy. He seemed to cope very well when it came to battling with the others for crumbs. Mo saw where I was looking.

'Wish they'd let me at 'im,' she said. ''E wouldn't have that leg, either.'

I wasn't paying much attention to her. Eventually she nudged me.

'You going anywhere tonight?'

'That'd be telling.'

'I'm going babysitting,' she said.

'Big deal,' I answered, trying to work out whether or not it was some sort of threat.

I didn't think it was a joke, I decided to take Sal out, to be safe.

We'd only got a few bob between us that night, and both families were staying in, so we decided to go for a wander round the estate and on into the woods.

We passed one or two hard nuts from our year. They were carrying bottles of cider.

'Looks like somebody's having a party,' I said to Sal.

We waved a few hand signals at them, and carried on our way.

At the next block, we passed a few more carrying bottles. We rounded the corner. There were about thirty kids outside the off-licence. They were mostly our year.

'Going to the party?' one of them asked.

'Party?' I asked.

'The party for the leavers.'

'Whose party?'

'Dunno,' he said, turning to his mate. 'Hey, whose party is it?'

'Who cares? Oh, hi there, Bean. Hello Sal. Why don't you come? It's for everybody.'

'Who says?' I asked.

'He did,' he said, pointing to another mate.

'Didn't so,' that one said. 'He did.'

He pointed to some guy at the other end of the crowd.

'Well, somebody did,' the first one said.

'Where is it?' I asked, panic beginning to rise in my voice. Was Mo doing an action replay? With a full cast.

'Corner of Dinmore. With the red door.'

I sighed with relief. It wasn't Sal's place.

'Who lives there?' I asked Sal.

Then I realised. I turned to Sal. She'd got a knowing look on her face.

'Hey,' I said, 'Isn't that where Mo baby-sits?'

Sal laughed out loud.

'Yes,' she said meaningfully, 'I know.'

I looked at her, understanding what she was telling me. She's got a head on her has Sal.

We didn't go to see the fun, but we heard about it all weekend. It seemed that Mo had been glad to see the first two, but by the time the thirty-eighth had arrived the welcome wore thin. Some decided to take their disappointment out on Mo, and the others decided to have the party anyway. The ones who couldn't get in, settled for having it in the front garden – until the police arrived. About then, the people who lived there turned up. What upset them most was that their kids had joined in the party, and their seven year old was plastered!

By Monday, all the school knew about it. Mo was letting on that she planned the party, but it had got out of hand. We didn't contradict her. She seemed to think I'd planned it. I didn't contradict that, either. It was no skin off my nose, and it was safer for Sal. But Mo's never forgiven me.

Sid and Dougie were annoyed that they'd missed 'Mo's party'.

'It's all your fault,' they said to me.

'She'd have invited us, but for you going out with Sal.'

'How come?' I asked.

'Well, she fancies you, that's what,' Dougie said.

'Ger off!' I said.

'She does.'

I hadn't thought of it like that, till then. It seemed funny to think that there might be people fancying you, and you not knowing about it. I quite liked the idea, till I remembered it was Mo we were on about.

Mind you, it must be hard on Mo. When she fancies boys they run a mile, because they think she'll bash their brains in. Poor old Mo.

Knockouts

General Editor: Josie Levine

Cassette tapes, with readings from the books, are available
for the following:
The Marco File read by Robert Powell
Save The Last Dance For Me read by Valentine Dyall

Stranger Than Tomorrow   read by Edward Petherbridge
The Six   read by Tony Robinson
The Six: Getting By   read by Michael Burlington and Anthony Hyde
The Six: Turning Points   read by David Goodland and Brian Hewlett
*A Northern Childhood: The Balaclava Story
   and other stories*   read by George Layton
A Northern Childhood: The Fib and other stories
   read by George Layton
Long Journey Home   read by Guy Gregory and Valerie Murray
Odysseus Returns   read by Christian Rodska
The Robe of Blood   read by Jill Balcon
The Bakerloo Flea   read by Michael Rosen
You Can't Explain Everything   read by Miriam Margolyes